PARENTS OF THE WORLD, UNITE!

HOW TO SAVE OUR SCHOOLS FROM THE LEFT'S RADICAL AGENDA

Ian Prior

CENTER
STREET

NASHVILLE   NEW YORK

Copyright © 2023 by Ian Prior

Cover design by Jay Smith-Juicebox Designs
Cover copyright © 2023 by Hachette Book Group, Inc.

Center Street
Hachette Book Group
1290 Avenue of the Americas, New York, NY 10104
centerstreet.com
twitter.com/centerstreet

First Edition: March 2023

Center Street is a division of Hachette Book Group, Inc.
The Center Street name and logo are trademarks of Hachette Book Group, Inc.

The Hachette Speakers Bureau provides a wide range of authors for speaking events. To find out more, go to www.hachettespeakersbureau.com or call (866) 376-6591.

LCCN: 2022949009

ISBNs: 9781546004448 (hardcover), 9781546004462 (e-book)

Printed in the United States of America

LSC-C

Printing 1, 2023

To my parents, John and Cheryl, for raising me to follow the courage of my convictions.

To my wife Elsie, for unequivocally supporting me through the long days and nights of following the courage of my convictions.

To my daughters Ava and Caroline, for motivating me to cross the Rubicon and stand up for my convictions.

CONTENTS

CONTENTS

THE BREAKING POINT

was standing on a sidewalk in Leesburg, Virginia when I first saw the video.

I'd been on the street for a few hours by that point knocking on doors. It was hotter than hell out there, and my T-shirt was soaked with sweat.

It was June 22, 2021, a day that would soon go down in Loudoun County history.

For me, it had been a day well spent. For three months, a group that I'd started, Fight for Schools, had been engaged in a campaign to unseat several members of the Loudoun County School Board. With the backing of dozens of parents (mostly moms), we were digging deep into the rot inside the leadership of Loudoun County Public Schools. From critical race theory to gender ideology to a Facebook enemies list, Loudoun County's parents were flooding school board meetings, sending Freedom of Information Act requests, and going on television and radio after viral moments during public comment sessions. Most consequently, however, we had launched a campaign to remove six school board members after they were caught being part of a private Facebook group called "The Anti-Racist Parents of Loudoun County." That group was plotting to cancel dozens of Loudoun parents who dared to speak at school board meetings in opposition to its draconian lockdowns and woke policies.

Today, I had been out collecting signatures for our removal petitions, which would ultimately have to be filed in court in a convoluted process where the odds were completely stacked against the petitioners. There was a school board meeting that evening that we knew was going to be intense. The board would be debating Policy 8040, which would allow biological boys to use girls' restrooms and locker rooms, and vice versa. It would also require teachers and students as young as five years old to refer to other students by their preferred pronouns.

Over 250 people had signed up to speak, mostly in opposition to the policy, but we sensed trouble, maybe even a setup by the school board to paint their opposition as insurrectionists. Having become the face of the opposition movement against the school board, I decided that I would take as many key team members as possible and go collect signatures while the meeting was going on.

The message? We weren't going to play their game. We wouldn't fall into their trap. Instead, we would go out and do the hard work of going door-to-door in Leesburg, Virginia, collecting signatures to remove school board members.

Looking down at my clipboard after returning home, I marveled at the number of signatures I'd been able to get, especially since I've never been a super-friendly, "knock-on-doors" kind of guy.

But as I suspected, the school board meeting turned into an utter disaster. The meeting was cut short after sixty-two speakers, two men were arrested, and the national and local media were running with the "insurrectionist right-wing parents" narrative. I thought it was very possible that our young movement had just screwed up big-time.

Watching the film of the school board meeting being played on the news was tough. It showed a man of about fifty arguing with a woman in a pink rainbow T-shirt. She was sticking her finger in the man's face while berating him about something. I could hear the phrase "That's not what happened" and the word "bitch."

Then a police officer come up behind the man, laying a firm hand on his shoulder. When the man pushed back, the officer went after him. After a few seconds of *Cloverfield*-style shaky cam action, they were down on the floor wrestling with each other. Within seconds, the man was sitting with his shirt pulled up over his stomach and his pants half down. There were knocked-over chairs all around him, and a crowd had gathered to take pictures.

It was a sad image, made sadder by the defeated look on the guy's face.

Soon, I knew, that image (not to mention the video footage I was watching) would be on every nightly newscast, newspaper front page, and Twitter feed in the United States.

In other words, we were screwed.

After taking a quick breather, I rewatched the video. On a second viewing, I heard another voice—a woman, her voice barely audible, shouting over the shutter clicks and shouts of horror in the room.

"This is what happens," she yelled. "My daughter was raped in school, and this is what happens!"

For a few seconds, I had no idea what to think.

Over the past few months, largely thanks to the work of Fight for Schools, these Loudoun County School Board meetings had become must-see television, and not only for parents in Loudoun County. As parents took to the podium to speak out against school closures, mask mandates, and some of the insane left-wing ideologies that were being pushed in our children's classrooms, the nation slowly learned that there was a revolution happening—and it wasn't going to stop in our small community.

I posted several of these speeches online. Many of them went viral, and for good reason. Parents around the country had spent the last year being told that they should have no say in what goes on in the classrooms of their children. They were told that lockdowns and school closures were necessary to stop the spread of Covid-19 despite overwhelming evidence to the contrary—not to mention the mountains of research showing all the psychological damage that would befall children who were kept away from their peers.

We were ticked off, and we weren't going to take it anymore.

All the while, members of the school board mocked us, ignored us, and spread rumors about us on social media. Just

4

a few months earlier, my name had ended up on the ene-mies list of a group called The Anti-Racist Parents of Loudoun County because I wrote an article opposing critical race theory in schools and showed up to a single school board meeting to advo-cate for the First Amendment rights of teachers and students. Six of our school board members were in that group and, despite learning of the enemies list as it was happening, did nothing to stop it. Even when the activities of this group became national news, the school board didn't say a peep. They didn't apologize, they didn't denounce the group, and most of them stayed in as the left-wing activists continued to plot against members of the community.

Clearly, the school board should have known they had just lit the spark that, if not carefully dealt with, could become a national parents' movement. But instead of skillfully unwinding the dam-age, they kept doubling down.

But in the days leading up to the infamous school board meet-ing, I could sense a change in the weather. For months, the board had been quietly planning to pass Policy 8040. According to this policy, boys who put on skirts and said they were girls could walk right into the girls' bathroom and use it, and any teacher who attempted to intervene could face disciplinary action. Even scar-ier, parents wouldn't have the right to know about their child's claimed gender identity at school unless the child gave staff per-mission to tell them. Given that the school was already packing the libraries full of books encouraging kids as young as five to question whether they were really boys or girls, this was a serious problem.

The school board knew that most parents in Loudoun County

were concerned, to put it mildly, about this policy. They worried for the safety of their daughters, who might find themselves in bathrooms and locker rooms with biological males with bad intentions. They also questioned the general sanity of passing such a policy. Hundreds of parents would show up to protest the new law at this meeting, which would be broadcast all over the country.

So the school board made plans to pack the room. In the days before the meeting, they asked for donations online so they could bus in transgender activists and left-wing protestors from across the state of Virginia. By the afternoon of the meeting, the parking lot of the school board building looked like the site of a football game or a Rolling Stones concert.

Luckily, I decided to stay away. I mistakenly thought we would be outnumbered and figured we should zig when they thought we would zag. But many on the team still wanted to go, so we decided to split up with about twenty people going to collect signatures. We knew that with that many heads butting at the same time, the meeting was a powder keg about to explode. Something bad was going to happen; it was only a matter of when—and, more importantly, which side would start it.

Now, having watched the video of this middle-aged man three or four times, I was sure that we—meaning the parents who'd showed up to protest Policy 8040—had screwed everything up.

What I didn't know was the whole story. In the days to come, I would find out that the man who'd been tackled was a local plumber named Scott Smith and that the woman yelling in the background of the video was his wife, Jess. On May 28, his daughter *had* in fact been raped in school, in the girls' bathroom, by a boy wearing a skirt.[1] If any parent at the meeting had raised the possibility of this happening, they'd have been denounced as a bigot and a monster before they could even finish speaking. But it had happened, and the school system was covering it up. When the next school year began, Loudoun County Public Schools had quietly moved the boy who'd assaulted Smith's daughter to another school, where— surprise, surprise—he would soon assault yet another young girl, this time in a classroom.[2]

Of course, I didn't know any of that at the time.

All I knew was that this meeting had gone up in flames exactly as I had feared, and it looked like my side—a group of dedicated parents who only wanted to fight for what was best for our children— was going to get blamed for it.

I was right.

Within weeks, we would be facing the ire of every news organization in the country. We would be bombarded with messages asking if our cause was worth it.

And, in a twist that *no one* expected, parents like me would be labeled as potential domestic terror threats by the Department of Justice under President Joe Biden. But then the pushback from the left boomeranged on them, and our cause would take center stage during a gubernatorial campaign in Virginia and even Congressional oversight hearings.

I'm sure that by now, you're probably wondering how I, a lawyer and former spokesman for the United States Department of Justice, ended up in this position. If this were a television show, this is the part where the record would scratch, the screen would freeze, and I'd turn to the camera with a big dumb look on my face to say something corny like "You're probably wondering how I got here."

Well…strap in.

Because it is a *wild* story.

THE RULES

I f you're reading this book, chances are you're interested in starting a parents' revolution in your own school district or neighborhood. What follows are twelve essential and battle-tested strategies for fighting back against your school's implementation of critical race theory, radical gender ideology, and the political agenda du jour that the Educational Industrial Complex is putting into school with your tax dollars paying the bills. Each chapter focuses on a single rule that any parent can use to successfully fight the radical woke agenda in their hometown. I'll use stories from my own activism to demonstrate how these strategies have worked.

Remember that in the beginning, the task can be daunting. No one likes talking to strangers or drawing attention to themselves, especially if that attention is going to put you in the line of fire. But if you find a good group of people, put your heads together, and keep your eyes on the prize, there's very little you won't be able to accomplish.

And if your goal is about something *other* than holding your school district accountable, you might benefit from these rules, too.

It's my firm belief that they'll work for anyone who wants to make change happen while making some friends along the way.

And don't worry. It's not like these are the rules of Fight Club. You can talk about them all you want.

RULES FOR STARTING A PARENTS' REVOLUTION

1. **Every Neighborhood Is a Battlefield.** Pay attention to what happens on your street and in your community. The infection of cancel culture and wokeism is not limited to the federal government, corporate boardrooms, professional sports, or Hollywood but has arrived next door. Be wary, but don't be afraid to get in the fight for the sake of your kids.

2. **Activate, Investigate, Communicate.** Every parent can be a private investigator into the moral corruption of the schools that they pay for and send their children to. With key tools like the Freedom of Information Act, the Protection of Pupil Rights Amendment, social media, and targeted media outreach, anyone can start to shine the spotlight of accountability on what is happening to their children in public schools.

3. **Always Flip the Script.** With a combination of fearlessness and humorous mockery, parents can punch through the far left's most potent psychological tool—fear of cancel culture—and bring the fight to the bullies.

4. **Identify the "Bad Guys" and Take It to 'Em.** Every conflict by its nature needs a good versus evil framework. But a neighbor versus neighbor fight on cancel culture

will not have the kind of long-term implications that can make meaningful change. It is therefore important to find the right "bad guys" to fight. Equally as important, however, is to identify your strategy and not let distractions shift your focus.

5. **Turn Your Fight into Must-See TV.** You cannot inspire in the darkness; you cannot pressure the enemy without the pressure of bad publicity. The greatest generals in history always knew that there must be an element of showmanship to the battle.

6. **Do Not Get Stuck in the Mud.** Always be in motion. The opposition, however clumsily, will start to fight back and try to engage you on their terms. Do not fall into the trap. When they zig, you must zag and keep moving forward to your goal.

7. **When They Mobilize, Go Guerrilla.** When you're going up against the status quo, they will find a way to mobilize their political power and legacy media. That's inevitable. What's *not* inevitable is how you respond. When they finally confront you in the air, morph into a guerrilla operation that maneuvers on the ground.

8. **Do Not Stop at the Wall.** A battle will have ebbs and flows, but at some point, you will find yourself hitting a wall. External and internal dynamics will make it challenging to get past that wall into the green fields on the other side. When you inevitably hit that wall, explode through it.

9. **You've Gotta Believe.** All the creative ideas, strategies, and tactics mean nothing unless you believe in your

cause and believe that you can win. Be flexible and open to ideas, but never take your eyes off the North Star and never forget why you joined the fight in the first place. Only then can you find yourself in the endgame you were destined to win.

10. **Don't Let 'Em Off the Ropes.** Eventually your strategies and tactics, if well executed, will bring you to a moment when your opponent is on the ropes. They've made crucial mistakes to be in that situation. When this happens, it's not time to back off. It's time to go for the knockout.

11. **Don't Be Overly Reliant on Past Success.** The greater the success, the greater the dangers that follow. Complacency will often set in as will the tendency to overly rely on the strategies and tactics that brought victory. Eventually your opponents will adapt to your tendencies and will exploit any signs of arrogance, impatience, and repetition.

12. **Play the Endgame.** Always know your endgame and always operate with that endgame in mind. Understand that what started as your primary goal may become subsumed into something much greater than you could have imagined. When it comes time to shift to that greater purpose, let your opponents distract themselves with what they think they know and where they think they can win while you silently redeploy your efforts to the final victory.

RULE NO. 1

EVERY NEIGHBORHOOD IS A BATTLEFIELD

KEY LESSON: Pay attention to what happens on your street and in your community. The infection of cancel culture and wokeism is not limited to the federal government, corporate boardrooms, professional sports, or Hollywood but has arrived next door. Be wary and don't be afraid to get in the fight for the sake of your kids.

HAPPY HALLOWEEN

Now, to explain how I ended up on a sidewalk with a few other parents on the verge of being labeled a potential domestic terrorist threat by Joe Biden, I'll have to take you back to another crazy scene that unfolded a few years earlier. Bear with me—we'll get to the school stuff shortly, but I'd never even have gotten there if things hadn't gone upside down in my neighborhood first.

It was Halloween night of 2018, and I was standing in a friend's living room dressed as Jesus Christ. I had the wig, the robe, the sandals, even a nice fake beard covering my all-natural beard to tie

13

the whole ensemble together. Looking at me that evening, standing between the fall-themed drinks and a few bowls of day-old candy corn, you'd have thought I walked right off the set of *Ben-Hur* and into this small, friendly neighborhood party.

For a few minutes, things were good. I stood talking to my buddy Chris from next door, who'd come dressed as a thinner version of Santa Claus. I had a beer, and we watched a bit of the World Series between the Red Sox and the Dodgers.

Then, suddenly, I heard a voice from behind me. I hadn't been dressed as Jesus long enough to think it was the voice of God, so I turned around.

And there, standing in a full-body koala-bear costume, was Ashley, a woman who would soon become my neighborhood nemesis (or one of them, at least).

In the eighteen months or so that I had lived in Loudoun County, Ashley had always been relatively friendly to me. She was known around the neighborhood as "The Organizer," and people tended to defer to her when it came to social events. She hosted an annual Christmas party, for instance, that always went way over the top. It was the kind of party that wives would look forward to for months and their husbands would grumble about because they weren't allowed to turn on the football game during party hours.

Ashley and her husband also had three kids, two of whom were the same age as my daughters. She ran an afterschool program called "Odyssey of the Mind," which we forced my oldest daughter to attend to help Ashley fill out the class. On the occasions that I ran into Ashley while I was picking up my daughter, she'd always smile, wave, and ask how things were going.

From the moment I saw her standing in front of me, a drink in her hand and two floppy koala ears drooping from either side of her head, I could tell that this interaction would be different, to say the least.

"I heard from Christy that I should talk to you about Brett Kavanaugh," Ashley said.

Damn, I thought.

Christy was one of my closest friends on the block. She had a great sense of humor, and I could tell that sending Ashley over was probably her idea of a joke.

Like Ashley, Christy was a liberal Democrat. She'd voted for Obama twice and Hillary Clinton once. But unlike Ashley, she hadn't completely gone off the liberal deep end. She may not always have agreed with me, but at least she respected that it was possible to be a decent human being while not buying into the idea that children could change their gender at will, for instance, or that teachers should hand out copies of the *1619 Project* and do lectures on white supremacy on the first day of third grade. To my knowledge, she hadn't run out and tried to burn down buildings when she learned that Donald Trump had won the election of 2016.

This, as I would soon find out, made Christy a rare beacon of sanity in Loudoun County, Virginia—a place that was growing more and more insane by the second.

I turned to Ashley and said hello and asked (very politely, I think) what specifically she wanted to talk about. Looking back, I'm sure you can chalk my pleasant tone up to the costume. It's hard to be confrontational when you're dressed as our lord and savior.

But it was no use.

For the next two minutes or so, Ashley ripped off a stream of leftist propaganda that was the worst combination of Rachel

Maddow, Keith Olbermann, and one of the real housewives of New Jersey. I'd just spent the past few hours at every picked-over Party City in the county trying to find a costume for this damned party, and this was not the way I wanted to get things started. As I stood holding my first beer of the evening, Ashley went on and on (and on and on and on) about how Brett Kavanaugh was a sexist, chauvinistic, angry drunk who had no place on the Supreme Court. She had clearly bought into the left's narrative about how he was a gang rapist who had victimized women and might victimize more, and asked how I could support his nomination. I told her I thought that even though this was a confirmation hearing, as opposed to a courtroom drama, he at least ought to have due process and some standard of proof beyond "just believe all women." She did not like that answer one bit!

Allow me to back up for a second. You see, it's not like this idea that I was best buddies with Brett Kavanaugh had come out of nowhere. For about seven years, I had been in politics. Republican politics. I ran a congressional campaign in Rhode Island for the former head of the Rhode Island State Police, worked at the National Republican Congressional Committee and American Crossroads, and eventually worked my way up to a job as Principal Deputy Director of Public Affairs in the Department of Justice under Attorney General Jeff Sessions.

On occasion, I would get a call from a producer at Fox News who thought I might have something interesting to say about current events, and I would oblige. I'm not saying that going on television was my favorite thing in the world, but the lawyer in me always enjoys arguing my point when I believe I've got the facts on my side. Most of my hits at that time had to do with legal issues related to the Department of Justice, but occasionally I would stray into the social side of things.

The previous month, just before the Kavanaugh hearings in September, I had been a guest on Fox News to predict how things would go. I appeared on Fox News exactly one time to discuss the nomination. *One.* And there was no way Ashley had even seen it (unless, of course, she'd taken the time to search me out on YouTube). This was before the smear campaign had even begun. So I just highlighted his record and said that I thought he had a chance of getting confirmed with 53 or 54 votes.

That's it.

But that was enough to put me in a conversation with Ashley that I definitely did not want to be in—at least at a Halloween party in the middle of someone's house. In any event, I had been watching the hearings and following the chaos, so by the time I found myself getting lectured by Ashley in the living room of one of my friends, I knew enough about where the battle lines were set. I calmly and soberly told her that it's easy to throw accusations around in the court of public opinion, but I wasn't going to just believe or disbelieve an allegation based on what some senator or political hack says on CNN; instead, I would make my own decisions with the raw information and evidence that was reliable.

Now, it's worth dwelling on the Kavanaugh story for another page or so. In many ways, it's a grim foreshadowing of the events to come. For those of you who've managed to flush that horrible story out of your minds (congratulations, by the way), here are the SparkNotes:

For 12 years, Brett Kavanaugh maintained a stellar reputation as a judge. He worked in the White House under President George W. Bush and then as a judge for the United States Court of Appeals for the District of Columbia. Those of us who worked in Republican politics knew him as a mild-mannered man who was a textualist and strict constructionist of the United States Constitution. While some of us were hoping for a bolder pick like Amy Coney Barrett, Kavanaugh was viewed as the safe choice. When President Trump announced in July that he'd be nominating Kavanaugh to fill the second Supreme Court vacancy of his presidency, the nation greeted the news with a collective shrug of its shoulders.

...which, of course, lasted for about 10 seconds.

After realizing that they probably couldn't attack this nice, wholesome soccer dad on principle, Democrats in Congress started digging into his past—and I mean *way* into his past. (This is a treatment that the left would soon give me, too, so I can say from experience that it is...well, let's just say "unpleasant.")

First, they found a letter that a psychology professor in California had sent to Senator Diane Feinstein of California that alleged Kavanaugh—or, more probably, someone who kind of looked like him—had sexually assaulted her in high school. For the first few weeks of Kavanaugh's confirmation hearings, they kept this letter secret, only exposing it when the woman who'd written it, now identified as Christine Blasey Ford, did an on-the-record interview with *The Washington Post* telling her story.

When it became clear that Kavanaugh was going to be confirmed unless they threw a big Hail Mary, the Democrats unveiled the letter and went all-in on the sexual abuser narrative. Due to the momentum of recent campaigns such as #MeToo and #BelieveAllWomen, it worked. Within weeks, these lunatics had spread the kind of rumors that would have seemed outlandish even in a late-series episode of *House of Cards*.

According to the stories of several more accusers, the man now up for a Supreme Court seat was a horrid, first-ballot-hall-of-fame creep. As a young man, he had gone around to the homes of his friends, always drunk on beer, and engaged in strange, violent sex acts with women who did not welcome his affections. In a matter of days, you could hardly hear the word "Kavanaugh" without associating it with the term "serial rapist." There were accusers all over the place, each one less credible than the last. Unsurprisingly, Michael Avenatti, aptly named "Creepy Porn Lawyer" by Tucker Carlson, got in on the action (so to speak).

Of course, none of it was true. But by the time Kavanaugh went on television to proclaim his innocence, there was virtually no Democrat left in the country—certainly in Loudoun County—who didn't think he was unfit for the job.

Which brings us back to my friend's living room.

Eventually the conversation got to the point where Ashley was raising her voice. My wife and I had arrived at the party late, and most people here had already enjoyed several glasses of punch (or something stronger) before we arrived. Several people in the room who'd heard this very one-sided conversation started to make their way downstairs to the basement. For a second, I thought that I might pass this conversation off to my poor friend Chris, but then Ashley's husband Chad, dressed in a tiger outfit, walked over in what I hoped would be an attempt to de-escalate the situation.

He didn't. Instead, he joined in, and it was Jesus versus a koala and tiger.

"Look," I said when I finally felt a break in their stream of anger. "We're just not going to agree on this. You've got your opinion, I have mine, and I don't think that's going to be changing during this party."

I remember my words exactly, of course, because I was dead sober at the time (and, if I'm recalling correctly, not all that thrilled about it).

Eventually, after another minute of back-and-forth, I managed to slide my way out of the conversation. I pretended to be all excited about something that had just happened on the TV showing the World Series, slid over to the TV, and left Ashley and Chad alone to cool off. The conversation was super awkward and annoying, but I just let it slide; no use getting all spun up because someone has a different take on something, however wrong I thought that take was.

We never spoke about it again. In fact, that strange confrontation never seemed to affect how we treated each other. Ashley continued to attend the same parties as we did, and she managed not to berate me in public about my (pretty tame) political opinions over the wine and cheese. We even had a reasonable political conversation at a Christmas party a few years later despite some of the neighbors making some obscene, but hilarious, gestures with her friend's penis-shaped cookies and a full-length Barack Obama portrait.

For a while, I thought that maybe her little one-sided screaming match on Halloween would be an isolated incident. Maybe it was a small, insignificant blip in what would otherwise be a pleasant, uneventful life in the suburbs.

Looking back now, I realize it was a warning.

ENTER THE EDNA

For the past few years, mostly since the election of Donald Trump, political polarization in the United States was getting worse than it had ever been. People—primarily liberals—were retreating into their partisan echo chambers, only hearing the news that confirmed what they already believed before they started watching. Their news came from Facebook, Twitter, Instagram, and the short, context-free videos that come up on those platforms. As a result, people retreated further into their tribes than they ever had before. That allowed them to get more radical every day. Soon, they began to see anyone who disagreed with them even slightly as backward and evil.

For the first year and a half that I lived in Loudoun County, these events were mostly things we read about online and in newspapers. They didn't happen in our neighborhood, where we all hung out together at least once a week at barbecues, playdates, holiday parties, and dinners. The occasional argument would happen, of course, but these never became so ugly that people turned around at parties to watch them.

Around the same time that I got into my first argument with Ashley, another person—named Edna—moved into the neighborhood. She was in her fifties and had three kids in high school and a husband no one ever saw. She would always wave, and she was perfectly friendly when you saw her in the street.

But one night at a neighbor's backyard firepit with a bunch of the guys on the street, I was told that she used to be a town councilor in a nearby town and that she had recently moved to our street after resigning from her position. It was also revealed during that party that Edna had a Twitter account and had tweeted that there were Republicans in her neighborhood with "Don't Tread on Me" license plates while having illegal aliens cut their lawn. Unfortunately, her attempt at exposing hypocrisy backfired as it appeared that Edna was referring to the guy across the street, who was Iranian and cut his own lawn.

Boys being boys, we decided to tweak her a little, and a few of us ordered Join or Die colonial flags and flew them as a subtle joke. It was all in good fun. At one point, when Ashley and her family came by for a small get-together at my house, she questioned whether my flag was racist. I rolled my eyes internally and told her it was a Revolution-era flag designed by Ben Franklin to bring more unity to the colonies during the French and Indian War and was used in the opening scene in the HBO series *John Adams*. I gave a cockeyed look at her, said "no," and she huffed her way into our house.

I thought to myself that maybe that Halloween incident wasn't isolated and that I should be very careful around her. But a bunch of us hung out on our back deck, and everything seemed to be friendly and fine.

It stayed that way for a while. Yes, Ashley and her friends tried to do LGBTQIASFL+- parades in the neighborhood and constantly posted pictures on Facebook showing how woke they were, but whatever—it didn't bother me. To each their own.

Politically, the left was ascendant in Loudoun and the country. Yes, Kavanaugh was confirmed, but Democrats won a majority in the House of Representatives in the 2018 midterms.

Meanwhile, in Loudoun County, a vacancy in the school board resulted in that public body shifting from a 5–4 Republican majority to a 5–4 Democrat majority at the end of 2018. The anti-Trump wave continued into 2019, where Democrats in Loudoun County took control of the Board of Supervisors and extended its majority on the school board to 7–2 and a candidate named Buta Biberaj as Commonwealth Attorney—the county's version of district attorney. Biberaj had won by a slim majority, aided by a last-minute donation of close to $1 million from George Soros.

Of course, I wasn't paying attention to any of this. A friend across the street—Jessica Mendez—had told me in the fall of 2019 that I should pay attention to the school board elections. Loudoun County Public Schools was in the process of stocking its libraries full of controversial books in the name of "diversity." Book titles included *My Princess Boy*, *Prince and the Knight*, and *It Feels Good to Be Yourself*, the latter of which deals with kids as young as five whose parents let them decide if they are transgender, nonbinary, or gender fluid. Jessica told me that hundreds had shown up to the board meetings to voice their dissent and I should get involved. At that time, I was busy starting up my own public affairs practice where I could work from home full time; local politics, culture wars, and getting myself canceled were the last things on my mind.

So the 2019 elections came and went, and I didn't even think to go vote. I'd always voted in federal elections and for governor, but I didn't vote in or get involved in local issues.

The result was a school board with seven new members who had ridden into power on a wave of anti-Republican sentiment driven by an electorate in Loudoun that had been trending Democrat over the past several years as educated liberals moved west from Alexandria, Arlington, and Fairfax in search of more land for less money.

A mere 10 weeks after taking office, that school board would face a challenge that they never could have anticipated.

They didn't just fail to meet the challenge; they completely botched it every step of the way. And riding right alongside the school board clown car were the likes of Ashley and Edna.

FLAG WARS

In early March 2020, I was scheduled to head to Louisville, Kentucky, for my friend and neighbor John's 40th birthday. Covid had reached the United States, but the full panic had not yet begun. There was talk about canceling, but we figured that this might be the last trip for a while, so we should go live it up.

It was a phenomenal trip, and I ended up buying about 10 high-end bourbons that I figured would occupy my top shelf for at least a year. After I returned, I was sipping some Angel's Envy rye while talking to my wife Elsie in the basement after the kids went to bed. I checked the news on Twitter and saw that Tom Hanks had Covid.

"Wow," I told Elsie. "This is going to be a big deal. Once you get a major celebrity with Covid, people are going to panic."

But it was 10 minutes later when I knew the world was about to change—the NBA indefinitely suspended its season. That meant billions in lost revenue for the NBA and the television networks. Certainly not something that should be taken lightly. I told Elsie that our kids were not going to be going to school for a while. She didn't believe me, but the next day we got the call that school had been canceled. Our daughters wouldn't set foot in a classroom for another 12 months.

I'm not gonna lie; being a student of history, I worried that we were looking at a bubonic plague situation, maybe the 1918 influenza outbreak if we were lucky. We ended up having dinner that Saturday with our friends. I was far and away the most militant about being super careful and staying in quarantine. Ultimately, we all decided that we should not continue to hang out at each other's houses and should allow kids to ride bikes outside only and that when the adults got together, and we would maintain some distancing.

So when word got out that Ashley yelled at a group of 10 people inspecting someone's new deck, I sort of understood her concern, even if her methods were way over-the-top.

By early May, however, people started to relax. No one was working in offices, people knew more about Covid, and everyone started accepting that this virus would be around for a while and you couldn't isolate forever. As a result, our neighborhood became a pretty normal oasis where people got about their lives.

While most of the neighborhood was getting on with their lives, Ashley was posting a day-by-day Facebook diary of her family's isolation. Again, to each their own. We were all a little amused by it to be honest. Pop on Facebook, see 45 pictures a day from Ashley's Daily Quarantine Log. It was annoying virtue signaling, but her social media behavior would soon take a turn that would ultimately be the catalyst for the parents' movement that swept the nation in 2021.

That turn came in May 2020 when George Floyd was killed by police in Minneapolis. I saw the video along with the rest of the world, and I was horrified by it. But being a rational person, I knew that Floyd's death—however horrible it was—was a vanishingly rare occurrence in the United States, where somewhere around 300 people of color were killed by police in the year 2020.

When Fox News asked me to pen an op-ed about the killing, I wrote that, based on what I saw, federal prosecution against the officer was appropriate. It was an op-ed that even the most liberal of my neighbors should have appreciated.

"From 2007 to 2011," I wrote:

I worked at the city of Boston Corporation Counsel's office defending police officers in civil claims of excessive force, wrongful conviction, and other lawsuits alleging constitutional violations. My natural inclination from that experience is not to rush to judgment in these kinds of cases, but to learn all the facts and see it from both sides before making a conclusion.

The George Floyd case is different. There is no nuance here. Surveillance video from a nearby restaurant makes it crystal clear that Floyd was handcuffed and appeared to be fully cooperative with police. The video shows there was no need for Minneapolis Police Officer Derek Chauvin to push his knee into Floyd's neck for eight minutes, ultimately killing a restrained and defenseless man.[1]

But takes like that were rare, as the country descended into protests, billions of dollars in property damage, and a new commitment from some to being "anti-racist." If you choose not to care about someone's skin color, do not see racism in all of our institutions, laws, and traditions, and are not working every day to end this systemic racism, then you must be named and shamed until you convert—according to these "anti-racists."

As you might have guessed, Ashley immediately dove headfirst into this activist mentality. On social media, she and her friends routinely slammed the police, Trump voters, and anyone who was not making enough of a commitment to "end racism." Which of course would be great, but there's a large contingent of us who think the best way to do this is simply to treat everyone the same, regardless of skin color, and continue to progress toward a nation where there is truly opportunity for all—something that requires a far more sophisticated approach than just calling everyone racist.

Ashley's Facebook activism eventually worked its way beyond Facebook and onto the street—quite literally. She decked her house out in Black Lives Matter swag and tried to organize a neighborhood driveway chalk drawing memorializing Floyd and denouncing racism. Mind you, the children in the neighborhood were mostly between the ages of four and seven, didn't know who George Floyd was, didn't know what racism was, and were more interested in running through the sprinklers than driveway chalk social justice. When one neighbor did a chalk drawing that did not condemn systemic racism strongly enough, Ashley—as this neighbor, who was a liberal and a friend of Ashley's, would later tell me—"was not happy" with her.

But none of this neighborhood virtue signaling was that big of an issue until a group of Willowsford residents had engaged in a campaign to convince our homeowners' association to change the name of a nearby body of water called Julia Jackson Pond. In their opinion, the name of this little pond was racist because it was named after Stonewall Jackson's mother, who was born right near the pond. Shortly after the HOA made the decision to rename the pond as a result of this under-the-radar campaign, this group of activists started posting about their victory in the community Facebook pages. It was really the first most people had even heard about this campaign. Personally, I wouldn't have changed the name, but the actual name change was not what ticked me off. It was that the homeowner's association, which the whole community pays for, decided to wade into the culture wars without putting it up for a community vote or even informing the community what it was considering beyond a vague "pond name change" in the agenda.

By then, it was too late to stop the "Julie Jackson Pond" from being renamed "Chorus Frog Pond," but many in the community were outraged by what seemed to be a secretive plan to enact social justice to the exclusion of 99 percent of the residents. Many of us wondered what was next. Were they going to take down the new name next year when people start saying that frogs are symbols of white supremacy?

Within a few days, people who'd been angry about the pond changing had formed into a new group of friends. This group consisted of several members, but three people in particular would come to play a major role in the coming fight: Darris and Beth, who lived up the street, and Stacy, who lived a few streets down. We chatted about different issues in the community and the county, and it was then that I first learned about the beginnings of a major uprising of parents against Loudoun County Public Schools.

In June, then-Superintendent of Loudoun County Public Schools Eric Williams announced a plan to open schools in August for two days a week followed by a July announcement that schools would be full-time virtual for the 2020–21 school year. Parents were rightfully angry, and dozens started showing up at school board meetings and protesting this decision. But as was the case the summer before with the so-called "diverse books" initiative, I didn't get involved. It was clear that these decisions were largely political, with Democrat-run counties like Loudoun in Democrat-run states like Virginia keeping schools closed, perhaps to inflict maximum pain on President Trump's reelection chances while leaving children and parents as collateral damage.

In any event, I still wasn't ready to engage in local politics. I had spent 10 years as a political operative but had never personally put myself out there on any issue. If I wanted to do that, I'd run for office, and that was the last thing I wanted to do.

But again, Ashley would inadvertently push me from my natural instinct to not get involved.

It was late July, and I had seen a thin blue line flag while driving my daughter to a horseback-riding lesson for her birthday. It was actually the first time I had seen the flag, and I loved the color scheme and thought it would be a good addition to my collection of historic American flags. But I forgot all about it until a few weeks later when I had some friends on my front porch for some Saturday evening beers.

My friend Dave, who lives across the street from me and was there that night, was a Marine and a member of federal law enforcement for the Department of Homeland Security. I brought up the thin blue line flag, and we joked about getting one to even out the BLM flags on our street. By our count there were three, but one of the social justice warriors on our street would soon take her BLM swag down while she listed her house for sale. I guess social justice works better for virtue signaling, less so for turning a profit on your house!

We joked around that they were afraid that if they didn't, the woke mob would start spreading online rumors that they weren't "supportive enough of Black lives." It wasn't unlike the grocers and tailors who'd been forced to tack up party posters in the Soviet Union, desperately hoping that the party police would pass them by that day. Of course, blindly putting up the flags didn't always mean you were safe. During the worst of the rioting in Minneapolis, I'd read a few stories about Black shopkeepers in the city who'd put up Black Lives Matter signs on their storefronts only to have violent mobs smash them up and loot the places anyway.

In other words: bending the knee to the mob wasn't going to get us anywhere.

Having spent four years defending police officers in court, managing the campaign of Rhode Island's former top cop, and working for the Department of Justice, I had preeminent respect for the risks that members of the law enforcement community take every day when they leave their families to go to work. In fact, while at the Department of Justice I had to personally sign off on every letter sent by Attorney General Sessions to families of law enforcement officers who had died while on duty. It was heartbreaking every time.

So I told Dave that I'd fly a thin blue line flag if he did, to which he eagerly agreed. The next day, I ordered two fresh, beautiful thin blue line flags. They were hanging outside our houses by Monday evening.

That Friday, my wife got a text message from Ashley. This is what she wrote:

"I hope you will at least think about how that action is perceived by your neighbors—your minority neighbors in particular. Since I have been putting on community diversity events, many of our minority neighbors have reached out to me. On multiple occasions

I was thanked for speaking up and being an ally. Without skipping a beat, the next statement was that they felt uncomfortable and unwelcome living on our streets because of the flags that are flying. This is a direct response to the actions you and other neighbors have taken by flying those flags. I felt good knowing I could help curb those feelings with my actions. I really like you and your family. This is why I felt I should at least make you aware of the impact those actions have on minorities in our neighborhood."

Wow! So in the three days since Dave and I had hung a pro-police flag we had insulted the minorities on our street who had all reached out to Ashley? As far as I could tell, there was one minority family on my street and we were friendly enough for me to have no doubt that if they had an issue, they would have let me know, not Ashley.

The very same day, Dave got a text from Ashley's husband, Chad, which made the true story clearer. In this one, Chad told Dave that he had seen the flag the day before while walking to Edna's house to get bubbles. He went on to say that his "initial thought was pretty negative; are you anti-black lives matter, you don't get it, and things down that path." Chad then suggested in a show of unity that Dave fly a BLM flag for a week and Chad fly a thin blue line flag for a week.

I was sincerely amused by the contradictory stories. Ashley claimed that all these people had been approaching her about my flag. But Chad had only seen the flag yesterday while going to Edna's to get bubbles. Hmm, it sounded like Ashley and Chad were just looking for a story to show how virtuous they were and how horrible we were.

In any event, Elsie politely let Ashley know that I was the one that bought and hung up the flags and if they had an issue, they should just reach out to me.

They never did.

Ultimately, our thin blue line flags ended up opening the floodgates of people on our street who had had enough of the cop bashing and keyboard warriors on Facebook lecturing everyone on how they could be better people. Within a week, I saw that thin blue line flags had begun popping up all over the place. There were five more on my street alone and another four on the street connected to ours. This proved what I had long suspected: that most people in this neighborhood were not insane, but they were afraid. They were afraid because standing up to the mob, as we'd recently learned via a series of very high-profile cancellations, could mean the end of their careers or complete ostracization from the community.

It was all silly neighborhood games and rivalries at this point, but my radar was sufficiently attuned to something going on. Wokeness was spreading beyond Hollywood, Washington, D.C., and cable news. It was metastasizing in neighborhoods. If you weren't a social justice activist, you were a bad neighbor and a bad person.

THE WARNING

Reading this book so far, you might have gotten the impression that I'm a guy who enjoys confrontation. I'm not. I'd like nothing more than to spend my days with my family, going for a run, reading a good book, taking my kids to the movies, or watching football.

But I don't like bullies. And the people in my neighborhood who were going after their friends and neighbors for expressing their beliefs were acting like bullies. I wasn't going to stand for it.

My friend Jack, who lived one street over, also had put up a thin blue line flag. Chad had gone to his house to discuss this "issue" with Jack and told him that they had reached out to me, but I'd never responded. That was not true, and it kind of got me a little peeved. But rather than overreact, I reached out to Chad and Ashley, let them know that Jack had mentioned they wanted to chat with me, and offered to have them come by on the Sunday before Labor Day to talk. Chad was receptive, and we set a time.

But before that could happen, I was implicitly called out in a long Facebook post by Ashley, in which she said: "People are mad as hell when they keep seeing their fellow humans murdered, beaten, and treated like rabid animals. And if you don't see it, you need to do more, read more, listen more (to people of color) until you do see it. When people keep thinking the right thing to do is stand behind 'a thin blue line' of law and order and dismiss the anger right now, ignore that a problem exists, and refuse to realize that things need to improve, nothing changes."

I had just texted her and her husband that morning to have a civil discussion, and, of course, she was now taking to social media to take what could reasonably be interpreted to be a subtle shot. I decided to respond in the most measured way possible despite my anger:

I think that you will find that many of those who "stand behind a thin blue line of law and order" have ideas, life experiences, and beliefs that may surprise you; perhaps even remove certain preconceptions that you have about what people see, what they do, what they read, and who they talk to. It is unfortunate when people project their own versions of what is in the hearts of others based on the flag they fly or who they support in an election. This makes it less likely that those people will work together, find common ground, and achieve progress. Social media is a difficult place to have those conversations, as it lacks the nuance of face-to-face discussions where people can treat each other as humans and not mere avatars behind a computer screen. However, as I am one of those to whom you are likely referring, you know where I live and I would be more than happy to have a productive, in-person discussion to see how we can all achieve the goals we desire.

I was fully aware, of course, that the last time Ashley had "talked to me in person" about a political issue I had ended up getting the business in the middle of a Halloween party. But I figured it was worth trying again, if we did it in the daytime with no adult beverages.

I figured she'd either say something nice in return or double down. What I didn't expect was for her to delete my comment. I guess she couldn't handle a rational, measured response to her post.

On the day of this little summit, I saw Chad striding into my front yard alone. Seemingly, Ashley had sent him alone to do her dirty work. We talked for a few minutes about our differences. Chad was perfectly pleasant but was clearly of the belief that people's subjective perspectives were far superior to objective standards. He also was all talking points on the issue of law enforcement and Black Lives Matter. I gave him data and facts.

In other words, we got nowhere, as expected.

But we parted cordially. On his way out, though, I gave Chad some advice that I hoped would set in.

"I'm not trying to tell you what to do," I said. "But one of these days Ashley's social media habits are going to cause you guys a lot of trouble."

I had no idea how right I would prove to be.

ACTIVATE, INVESTIGATE, COMMUNICATE

KEY LESSON: Every parent can be a private investigator into the moral corruption of the schools that they pay for and send their children to. With key tools like the Freedom of Information Act, the Protection of Pupil Rights Amendment, social media, and targeted media outreach, anyone can start to shine the spotlight of accountability on what is happening to their children in public schools.

STEP ONE: ACTIVATE

By the summer of 2020, there were at least 10 stacks of old puzzle books in every room of my house. It was also during this time that the George Floyd riots dominated the news as well as the brains of neighbors like Ashley and Edna. But I never made the connection between woke neighbors and what was happening in the schools.

The first indication that something was wrong on an institutional level was a story in the *Washington Free Beacon*, a conservative media outlet. Someone had posted it on Facebook, and I took an interest in the story, written by a reporter named Chrissy Clark, who found that Loudoun County Public Schools were using something called the "Teaching Tolerance Program," which had been developed by a team at the Southern Poverty Law Center.

"Virginia kindergarten students will learn about institutional racism alongside the alphabet," the article read. "The proposed lesson plan recommends restricting history and social studies classes to emphasize slavery as fundamental to American society for students from kindergarten to the fifth grade."[1]

Aside from the obviously insane premise that students in kindergarten should learn that slavery remains "fundamental to American society," the mention of the Southern Poverty Law Center set off alarm bells in my head. For years, when I heard about the Southern Poverty Law Center, I pictured an organization full of brave, level-headed civil rights crusaders who had stood up to the Ku Klux Klan in Alabama and fought for the freedom of African Americans during the repressive Jim Crow era. I thought they were people who wanted to live up to Martin Luther King Jr.'s dream of a society where people would be judged based on the content of their character rather than the color of their skin.

But in recent years, that had all changed. The Southern Poverty Law Center became famous for its list of "hate groups," which turned every major organization that did not align with its leftist ideology into the modern-day incarnation of the KKK.

Wondering what everyone else in the community might think, I posted the *Free Beacon* article in one of our neighborhood Facebook groups. This was a place for parents to talk about afterschool activities, post homework tips, and discuss what was happening inside their children's classrooms. It certainly wasn't a place to have knock-down, drag-out political fights.

But since Covid and the killing of George Floyd, the rules had changed. Now, the left-leaning parents in my neighborhood believed that there was nothing in the world—cocktail parties, barbecues, a Facebook post—that couldn't be turned into a screaming match.

Almost as soon as I posted the article, Edna was writing full paragraphs in the comments. It was like she'd been sitting at her laptop all morning watching Ibram X. Kendi videos on YouTube, just waiting for someone to question the ideology of anti-racism. The talking points came quickly, and they didn't stop.

"That's not part of the curriculum," she wrote before claiming that the *Washington Free Beacon* was a questionable news source.

She also claimed that the program was designed only so that children could learn about the history of slavery, segregation, and the civil rights movement—something, she suggested, that local racists were trying to stop their children from learning about. So, if I was understanding her correctly, the "Teaching Tolerance Program" was (a) not something that kids were learning about in school and (b) extremely important for kids to learn in school, and if you didn't think so, you were a racist.

Now, I don't know about you, but I went to elementary school in blue Rhode Island between the years of 1982 and 1989, and I had absolutely no trouble finding out any of those things. My classmates and I learned all about slavery, the Civil War, post-war segregation, and the brave heroes of the civil rights movement who helped end it. As a history major and law school graduate, I understood these issues on a far deeper level, specifically how our institutions had failed to take action to root out discrimination until the mid-twentieth century. Yet these new, upper-class, white "anti-racist" parents were acting like those things had been state secrets for years, as if students filed into their classrooms every day to get lessons in white supremacy and why the South should have won the civil war. It was a false premise.

For a moment, I wondered whom Edna might have been talking about when she referred to the "local racists" who objected to teaching lessons about slavery and civil rights. But I didn't have to wonder long. Seemingly, she was referring to anyone who disagreed with her even slightly or who wasn't willing to fly BLM flags in their yard or spend hours a day doing chalk drawings of George Floyd. Obviously, this "woke" stuff—which, honestly, had seemed kind of silly at first—was quickly becoming a cult, and some of my neighbors seemed brainwashed. I didn't think we had long before their twisted ideology made its way into our school system.

Of course, I was a little late on that.

In late July 2020, I sat down at my kitchen table and attended my first Loudoun County School Board meeting. Given that we were still right in the middle of Covid, the whole thing was done over Zoom, which gave the proceedings an odd, impersonal feel.

Watching the little squares appear on the screen of my laptop, I realized that I wouldn't have known a single member of my school board if I had literally run into them on the street. I didn't know what they looked like, what their political affiliations were, or, to be honest, what they did all day. Like most parents in my neighborhood, I just assumed that they were looking after the best interests of the children in our community.

This, I would soon learn, is something you can never take for granted.

For the next two hours, I watched as these people batted around one insane idea after another. The whole thing felt more like a weird religious service than a school board meeting. First, they unveiled their "Detailed Plan to End Systemic Racism," talking about how they would change the names of schools, get rid of "racist" mascots, and issue an apology to the Black community on behalf of the school board, which did not desegregate until the late 1960s. I didn't see what any of this had to do with making sure my children got a good education in an actual classroom, but it seemed pretty harmless to me. At the worst, it was virtue signaling and wasting everyone's time.

Then they kept talking. About an hour into the meeting, they began talking about how there were not enough African American students being admitted to the "high-performing" Academies of Loudoun, which had been in existence for exactly two years by this point. These were schools that required students to take exams, meet certain metrics, and receive several recommendations to gain admission. For this one year that the Academies of Loudoun was in existence, the percentage of Asian students who gained admissions far outpaced their overall representation in the school population, while Black, white, and Hispanic students were underrepresented vis-à-vis their representation. Somehow, the Loudoun County School Board determined that this trend was due to white supremacy, and they could fix it by getting rid of rigorous testing and academic requirements and replacing them with...nothing, really. According to their plan, admission to high-performing schools in the county would be based on promoting "the racial and ethnic diversity of admitted students" despite the fact that Asian students made up the vast majority of admitted students.

This, they reasoned, was a way to foster "equity" in the community, which the school board believed was its sole responsibility after the Black Lives Matter protests that had been raging for months. I would soon learn that the word "equity," which sounded perfectly reasonable at first, was in fact one of the strangest and most sinister terms in the English language. It meant, effectively, that institutions should be reorganized until the racial makeup of those institutions was exactly where the far left wanted it—something that changed every day. It was no longer enough to make sure that all students were equally prepared for a magnet school entrance exam, for instance, or that their parents all had equal opportunity to apply for spaces in those schools. Now, any merit-based admissions process that did not produce the left's desired results was racist, and it needed to be eliminated forever.

The same went for discipline in schools. After realizing that non-white and non-Asian students tended to be suspended more often for in-school offenses, the school board decided that schools should no longer be allowed to suspend students for certain offenses. Once again, this whole project seemed backward to me. Rather than forcing all students, regardless of race, to meet the same standards, the school board was attempting to eliminate all standards in the name of "equity." Aside from being stupid, it also struck me as, to use the left's favorite word, racist.

If you eliminate a test because a Black kid might not perform well on it, you're effectively telling that Black kid that he or she is inherently less capable of preparing for that test than his or her white and Asian classmates. The answer, I thought, isn't to get rid of rigorous academic standards or to stop suspending all kids for certain infractions but to make sure that all children, regardless of race, were better prepared to meet those high standards. In other words, teachers should be doing their jobs and teaching real skills to give every student an equal opportunity rather than droning on for hours about equity and systemic racism.

Aside from my philosophical objections to these policies, they weren't going to work in practice. In normal times, that would have been clear to anyone who heard about them. But in the summer of 2020, with social justice warriors like Edna and Ashley combing every corner of cyberspace looking for people they could expose as racists, most parents were afraid to say anything. If a policy was presented as something that might have a positive impact on "equity"—a word few people in the United States at the time had even heard until a few days earlier—then that policy would move forward with an unlimited budget. Anyone who objected, in the view of the anti-racist parents of Loudoun County, was "perpetuating a system of racism and white supremacy."

After that meeting, I was "activated." Although that might sound like something out of *Mission Impossible*, it's pretty simple in the context of this story. A parent—or anyone—is "activated" when they look around at the world and realize that they are being gaslit. For some parents I know, it happened when they were called racists simply for questioning the wisdom of slogans like "all cops are bastards." For others, it happened when they were told that their children had to be separated by race in their classrooms so that they could learn vital lessons about systemic racism and equity.

If you've picked up this book, there's a good chance that it's happened to you already.

For the next few days, I put my puzzles and books aside and started looking into where all these wacky ideas had come from.

The question I wanted to answer was simple. What was the source of all these bad policies? Why was it that even though nearly every school district in the country was wrapped up in this business of equity, anti-racism, and education reform, the Loudoun County School Board seemed light-years ahead of them all when it came to bad, batshit-crazy ideas?

I had a hunch that all of it, somehow, came down to money and power. And I was determined to find out how much money, where it was coming from, and, if I was right, how to stop it.

Unfortunately for the children of Loudoun County, I *was* right—more than I possibly could have imagined.

STEP TWO: INVESTIGATE

If you want to get to the bottom of what is happening at your children's school, you have to be more than a parent. You have to turn into an investigator, because the school is not simply going to hand over the damning information in response to an email. I learned when I emailed the principal at my daughters' school about the *Washington Free Beacon* article about using politicized material from the Southern Poverty Law Center and they told me they denied using it.

But before you get down to investigating, you need to start with the end in mind. That's not to say you're going to have the results of that investigation beforehand, but you absolutely need to frame everything you are looking for in terms of explaining the who, what, when, how, and, most importantly, why. You may not get all those answers in one shot, especially the why. But you need to build your case so that, at the end, you can communicate exactly what you found in a manner that everyone can easily understand.

In this case, I needed to start with the who, what, when, how, and why. Who was pushing this on LCPS? What was the trigger for its Equity Plan and its Action Plan to End Systemic Racism? When did this start happening? How did this all go down? Most importantly, why did this happen? The answer was right there for all to see—an "equity report" relied upon by the Loudoun County Public Schools to implement a more woke view of the world.

As I would learn, equity audits are being conducted in schools across the country. Essentially, the school system will pay an equity consulting committee big money to come in, write up a report stating that the school has a "low level of racial consciousness," recommend some fixes, and suggest that the school division would be enormously helped by keeping the consultant under contract so that they can supervise these changes.

The first step, then, was to read the audit. If they were going to make outrageous claims about racism and a lack of "equity" in an entire school system based on one event, I wanted to see what evidence they had to back it up.

Unsurprisingly, there wasn't much. After an "investigation" that lasted approximately three months, during which consultants from the Equity Collaborative interviewed several anonymous teachers, staffers, students, and African American and Hispanic parents in Loudoun County (while excluding Caucasian and Asian parents), the company came back with a document that came to be known as the "Equity Collaborative Report." This report concluded, to the surprise of absolutely no one, that the school division was systemically racist and that they had lots of (expensive) work to do if they wanted to change that. They based their findings of systemic racism on anecdotal testimony by anonymous students and parents about specific incidents at school, but they did not verify the accusations or look at the other side of the story to determine what the truth was. My immediate thought about this report was that the "investigation" by the Equity Collaborative was one conducted with predetermined results.

They had been hired to deal with supposed issues of systemic racism and on the surface, their report seemed to have found it. However, even the laziest Psych 101 student could have looked at this document and realized that we were dealing with a classic case of "confirmation bias" that was qualitative and not quantitative.

In short, the report appeared to me as nothing more than woke, consultant speak without much in actual substance. That feeling was backed up when I did some quick research of the Equity Collaborative and found that one of their key trainings for schools was Introduction to Critical Race Theory.[2] In this presentation, the Equity Collaborative critiques ideas such as "color-blindness, the neutrality of the law, incremental change, and equal opportunity for all." The slides go on to claim that meritocracy—that those who maximize their abilities through hard work succeed—is systemically racist. It also defined "whiteness" as a "property interest" and stated that "racism controls the political, social, and economic realms of U.S. society."

With just a little thought and preparation, I had developed the outlines of a story. Woke consultant received money from Loudoun County Public Schools to consult on how to be...more woke.

The next question was why. Were the people at the Equity Collaborative friends with someone in the LCPS administration or a powerful figure in Loudoun County politics? I wasn't able to draw that connection, but I did have a thought on why this may have happened.

The trail began, oddly enough, in the gymnasium of Madison's

Trust Elementary School in Ashburn, Virginia. There, in February 2019, two gym teachers allegedly organized a "runaway slave game" for the kids in their class. According to a story in *The Loudoun Times-Mirror*, the game involved making some students "slaves" and others "slave owners" and then letting the owners chase the runaway slaves in a strange, twisted version of tag.[3]

Clearly, this was bad. Like, *very* bad. Of course, the truth was very different from the narrative that was sold to the press and that I bought into in August 2020, but that is for a different chapter.

Soon, the local branch of the NAACP got involved, and Loudoun County Public Schools started scrambling for anything that would keep them out of trouble. They agreed to create something called an Office of Equity, to form an Equity Committee on the school board, and to hire a consulting company to do an equity audit at the school. That consultant ended up being the Equity Collaborative, and its report was the inflection point that was driving the wokenization of Loudoun County Public Schools.

I had at least a surface understanding of the who, what, when, how, and why. But as with anything, it is money that makes the world go 'round and money that makes schools go woke. I had a hunch that the Equity Collaborative made enough off this endeavor to get people's attention—maybe six figures.

Luckily, parents have a secret weapon for finding out such information: Freedom of Information Act requests. In my opinion, all parents in the United States should know what these are, how to file one, and how to make sure you get the best results possible when you do.

Like most things involving the government, it's a little more complicated than you might think.

First, some background.

Passed in 1966, the Freedom of Information Act, or FOIA for short, allows any citizen of the United States to request records from any federal agency in the United States. There are exemptions for deliberative communications, national security information, and that which is covered by attorney-client privilege. But at the federal level, FOIA is a godsend for investigative reporters trying to find government abuse or misconduct.

Each state also has its own version of the Freedom of Information Act that applies to state agencies and local governing bodies.

I had never submitted a FOIA before but had certainly sent my share of document requests and subpoenas as a lawyer, and it wasn't all that different. Most governments will have an electronic FOIA portal, which requires you to sign up with an email address and password. Once you're set up, it's just a matter of making narrowly tailored requests so that the government FOIA officer can easily get you what you're looking for. In this case, I simply asked for the contract between Loudoun County Public Schools and the Equity Collaborative as well as all invoices and payment records in 2019.

Here is the original text of that request. At the very least, it might serve as a template for any requests you'd like to file in the future:

- Any and all written communications, from January 1, 2019, to December 31, 2019, between LCPS and the and the Equity Collaborative, LLC.
- Any and all written communications, from January 1, 2019, to December 31, 2019, between LCPS and any other consultant retained by LCPS to perform an equity audit.

- Any and all source material used by the Equity Collaborative in preparing its June 6, 2019, report to Superintendent Eric Williams including but not limited to source records of the focus groups and interviews referenced on page 5 of the Equity Collaborative's June 6, 2019, report to Superintendent Williams.
- Any and all contracts between LCPS and the Equity Collaborative, LLC.
- Any and all written communications to, from, and between LCPS staff (including all of 2019 and 2020) concerning the adoption of curriculum recommended by "Teaching Tolerance" or Southern Poverty Law Center."
- Any and all contracts between LCPS and any other consultant retained to perform an equity audit.
- Any and all records of payment by LCPS to the Equity Collaborative, LLC.
- Any and all records of payment by LCPS to any other consultants retained to perform an equity audit.

After sending this request, I fully expected the school district to reject it on baseless grounds. There are nine ways that the government can do so, and the most popular one is for attorney-client privilege for when the school division's lawyer is one of the recipients of the email. If the government determines that the FOIA requests exempt information, then they can reject your request. They can also say that it would require too much time to pull together all the files you're looking for. Then, of course, they can just plead poverty, charge you a fortune, and take forever to get to your request while figuring out a way to use an exemption to redact all the valuable information.

If you look around the internet, you can find some pretty blatant instances of the government attempting to keep information from people who've filed requests via FOIA. Reporters will often post pictures of documents hitting their inboxes with all but one word redacted in thick black ink or of files that arrive on CD-ROMs that later turn out to be unreadable. One mom in Loudoun County sent a FOIA request for mentions of sexual assaults during a five-month period, and they quoted her a bill of $37,000.

But much to my surprise, the school district came back in five days, and what I saw shocked me. Reading through the contract and the related invoices, I was surprised to find that the Equity Collaborative had charged Loudoun County Schools $422,000 for their work in 2019 alone. I later learned that the Equity Collaborative remained on contract into 2021 at a rate of $625/hour.

My first investigation into Loudoun County Public Schools was complete. I had a story, and now I just needed to communicate it.

STEP THREE: COMMUNICATE

As a media professional, I knew when something would resonate as a national story and when it wouldn't. A local school division paying $422,000 to an educational consultant? Maybe that's a local story, but it's not a national story by itself. But the fact that this consultant was pushing critical race theory as a framework for schools? That was something much bigger.

At the time I received the contract between Loudoun County and the Equity Collaborative, the term "critical race theory" was just starting to generate buzz, and for good reason. While critical race theory has been around for decades, in both legal and educational scholarship, it was Nikole Hannah-Jones and her 1619 Project that really put it on steroids and launched it to prominence after her introductory essay in the August 2019 *New York Times Magazine.* The premise was that America's history of slavery was woven throughout our society and, thus, our very existence as a nation was tainted with irredeemable racism.[4] The media hyped her work to no end, and she even received a Pulitzer Prize for that introductory essay.

This wasn't a new line of thinking, and many of her concepts had been working their way from higher education to K–12, albeit subtly. There were no "critical race theory" lessons listed on a school's curriculum, but through teacher trainings and school "equity statements," it was clear that there was a new push to teach children as young as kindergarten that America's institutions, traditions, language, holidays, and very founding were all racist and must be disrupted and dismantled.

Over the past few years, a former documentary filmmaker named Christopher Rufo had been collecting stories about critical race theory diversity trainings in the federal government and reporting on them. Before long, he was the country's leading expert in what was known, largely thanks to his work, as "critical race theory."

But it was James Lindsay's appearance on the Joe Rogan podcast that was the first time I had heard this term, and I was fascinated. I later devoured his book *Critical Theories* and explored the roots of this new, woke way of thinking. After reading Matt Taibbi's blistering criticism of Robin DiAngelo's *White Fragility*, I plowed through that. I read key critical race theory–inspired authors like Ibram X. Kendi, Michael Eric Dyson, and Paulo Freire. I went into this experiment with an open mind and came out with a simple conclusion: this was all about people making money by preying on the white guilt of our woke neighbors.

That's not to say that there aren't serious socioeconomic issues in this country that lead to disparate results, but the idea that the rule of law, enlightenment rationalism, the Constitution, and equal opportunity theory all perpetuate systemic racism is a load of garbage.

Of course, by September 2020, the term "critical race theory" was on the minds of conservative thinkers and politicians. Much of that was due to Rufo, who was able to work with the Trump administration to get its attention on this issue and ban critical race theory trainings in the federal government and with government contractors.[5]

This meant that there was a national interest in critical race theory and I was sitting on a story where a Virginia school system shelled out nearly half a million to implement it. This was a local story with major national implications. Yet in the media everything is a matter of timing. With a presidential election and a Supreme Court nomination, it would be tough to get Fox News or other right-of-center platforms to run with this.

But there's more than one way to skin a cat. In my experience, I had always found that if you get a big story placed in a smaller publication and then push that story to bigger publications, they will often do their own version since the work has largely been done. A friend of mine ran a network of local news sites that was begging for stories like this. It just so happened that one of the sites—West Nova News—covered Northern Virginia. I pitched him the story, and a few days later it was published.

Then I went to work on Twitter, Facebook, and email, getting this story out everywhere. Eventually the *Washington Free Beacon* and our local ABC affiliate picked it up, as did several influencers on social media like Tom Fitton of Judicial Watch. The story may not have been highlighted by Tucker Carlson, but it was getting people in the community talking.

From there, I started to get some tips from people in the community who were involved in school-related issues. One of those tips came from a woman who had run for the school board in 2019. It was a proposed code of conduct that would subject LCPS staff to discipline for criticizing the school's commitment to equity, even if that criticism was made outside work during conversation. It also encouraged staff to report such violations, and it wouldn't punish staff for false reports. It was shocking and looked like something out of Soviet Russia.

I pitched that story as well, and the *Washington Free Beacon* reported it. Then I wrote an article for *The Federalist* detailing everything I had found between the Equity Collaborative and this new proposed code of conduct.

I had been activated. I investigated. Then I communicated. Now I was meeting different people who had been railing about LCPS for at least a year.

I eventually went to speak at my first school board meeting in October 2020. I was going to speak on the code of conduct, which was scheduled for a vote, but the community and even teachers' union outrage about that policy forced the school board to drop it. I ended up going in with a fiery speech about the First Amendment and then went home.

But then I stopped digging in. As is always the case when you're involved as a consultant with political campaigns (as I was in the fall of 2020), things slow down for about two months after an election before picking back up in January. I used this time to unwind, visit family, enjoy the holidays, and read as many books as I could before reengaging with work in January.

One of the books I read during that time was *Bleak House*, by Charles Dickens. I had started and stopped that book more times than I can count, but I was determined to read all 900 pages this time. There is one character in that book—Mrs. Jellyby—who was the Victorian Era version of today's virtue signaller. Mrs. Jellyby was all about social causes, particularly her "Boorioboola-Gha venture" in Africa. However, Mrs. Jellyby is so focused on her causes of virtue, that she fails to see how her own obsessions are hurting others.

I couldn't help but laugh and think of Ashley and Edna.

Fortunately, I had unfollowed their social media accounts, didn't have any contact with them, and thought, "hey, you can't be best friends with everyone on the street! No need to think about them anymore."

In essence, after my initial foray into what was wrong at Loudoun County Public Schools, I got distracted, deactivated, and went about my life.

As it turns out, the fight hadn't even started.

RULE NO. 3

ALWAYS FLIP THE SCRIPT

KEY LESSON: With a combination of fearlessness and humorous mockery, parents can punch through the far left's most potent psychological tool—fear of cancel culture—and bring the fight to the bullies.

#CANCELED

When I was working at the National Republican Congressional Committee as a spokesman during the 2014 midterm election cycle, my friend and boss Andrea Bozek used to say, "Always be on offense." But as a former lawyer who almost exclusively worked on the defense side on behalf of the police, I was never fully comfortable STARTING OUT on offense and firing away at everything and anything. Rather, my style was to wait, see the battlefield take shape in front of me, wait for my opponent to make a mistake, and then exploit it with withering, relentless, and targeted counterattack in a way that was unexpected. I had used that strategy with great success winning 15 trials, and I had used it while working as a political communicator in some of the most watched races in the country.

In March 2021, I would once more employ the counterattack strategy in a local fight that would end up becoming a national one.

As I mentioned in the last chapter, after my initial toe drop into the Loudoun County Public Schools fight, I ended up plugging into a small network of people who had been digging into Loudoun County Public Schools issues. I sat on a few calls and met some people for coffee and lunch, but I figured I'd serve as a resource for how they could be effective at their mission of making changes at LCPS. I didn't expect to be at the forefront of any fight and never expected that lingering animosity from a neighbor would force me headlong into a political battle for the history books.

But soon I would learn a valuable lesson: never underestimate the desire for revenge among the woke.

Luckily for us, the woke really only has one weapon, and it's already getting old. When someone says something that they don't like—or retweets something they don't like or fails to say something that they should have said or laughs at a joke they shouldn't have laughed at or commits one of a million strange offenses against "social justice"—a familiar routine happens. Members of the mob coordinate a campaign on social media to make sure everyone in the world knows what you did (or said or didn't say or laughed at and so on). This gives the illusion that somewhere in the world, there are millions of people who all want your head on a platter, even when the real number of people who actually care is probably closer to single digits.

But that's only the beginning.

Next, they'll dig through the archive of every statement you've ever made and every picture you've ever appeared in to try to find some more kindling to throw on their outrage bonfire. Once they find that, the volume of tweets and Facebook posts goes up exponentially. Thousands of people who log on to Twitter every day to get outraged about things—which, in the year 2023, is pretty much what the platform is good for—see the messages, retweet them, and add their own snarky notes to the top. Before long, your name is trending alongside a hashtag, and people are combing the internet to find out where you live, where you work (for now), and whether you've ever associated with any other "problematic" people.

This is when most people freak out, bend the knee to the mob, and apologize. They issue a press release that includes phrases like "deeply sorry for my actions" and "strive to do better" and then hope that'll be enough to stop the attacks from coming.

But when you're playing defense like that, it never does.

No apology and no defense are ever good enough for the woke mob. Once you're in their sights, they won't stop until you're completely shamed, fired, and probably living in a small shack in the mountains alone. I'm sure you don't need to think for very long before you come up with a few dozen examples of people who've been called out by the woke mob, tried to apologize, and still ended up losing everything.

Back in the early 2000s, the people this happened to were mostly public figures—well-known people who had made a conscious decision to live their lives in the public eye. Back then, you could understand them getting some backlash when they did things that displeased their audience. I don't think anyone batted an eye, for instance, when the famous Food Network personality Paula Deen was called out and "canceled" for some pretty serious accusations of racial discrimination. When the radio host Don Imus had his show taken off the air after he said something truly racist back in 2007, most normal people were perfectly fine with it.

But then came social media, which changed everything. Now, anyone who could gin up enough outrage was able to cancel people for anything that offended them personally. This led to the attempted cancellations of thousands of people, the vast majority of whom had done nothing wrong. When Stephen Colbert, who used to play a fake right-wing character on Comedy Central, said something racist against Asian people on television to make fun of people who were *actually* racist against Asian people, a few social media activists came pretty close to getting his show pulled off the air. Looking back on their hashtag, #CancelColbert, you can see one of the first uses of a word that we would all come to use every few hours in the years to come.

In a recent article titled "Why the Past 10 Years of American Life Have Been Uniquely Stupid," the psychologist Jonathan Haidt points out that the prevalence of "cancel culture" has very little do to with the actual issues that activists pretend to care about.[1] Instead, he reasons, it's all about gaining status in one's community. So, when you've got a bunch of woke people who believe everything is racist, according to this model, the best way for them to gain status among one another is to find as many racists, sexists, and homophobes as possible and call them out. Given that there's a finite number of *actual* racists, sexists, and homophobes in the world, these people have to go after smaller and smaller targets until they're finally going after their neighbors for committing "microaggressions."

By the late 2010s, this practice had become almost comical.

People were getting called out on social media for things they'd done 20 years ago, and they were apologizing for them as if they were class A felonies. It's no surprise that people like Ashley and Edna felt like they had the power to shut down anyone who disagreed with them.

They did.

Shortly after moving to Loudoun County, I had watched a real-life cancellation play out in my own backyard. The whole thing was chilling, mostly because of how commonplace it had become.

It started, as always, with an online activist looking for dirt. Early in the summer of 2020, with the nation engulfed by protests and riots after the killing of George Floyd, a local activist came across a picture of a T-shirt on Facebook. The shirt, which used to be sold at a place called Parallel Wine Bar in the Ashburn district of Loudoun County, said, "Drunk Wives Matter."[2]

Get it?

Like "Black Lives Matter," but...?

It was a joke...on a T-shirt. It wasn't racist or hateful. It was just a way for a small businessowner to make people laugh and bring in some extra money for his restaurant. But as the nation got "woke" in the summer of 2020, the owner of Parallel Wine Bar started to feel like maybe selling a shirt that took any kind of stance on Black Lives Matter was a bad move for business.

He stopped selling the shirt, pulled it from the restaurant's website, and hoped that would be the end of it.

It wasn't.

As soon as this angry woke activist saw it, she tweeted out the image with this message:

Just in case you live under a rock, this shirt is literally hanging
   on the wall at Parallel Wine & Whiskey Bar. And they make
   money off people buying them. The owners are straight
   up racists. Spread the world.
Derek- got one for ya . . . .

I'm sure I don't need to tell you what happened next.

Spurred on by all the national outrage, the woke, white subur-
banites of Loudoun County descended upon this unfairly maligned
wine bar with enough force to shake the earth. Apparently, "Derek"
was a guy who'd been keeping a list of "racist" online acts to feed
the left-wing outrage machine. And it was hungry. For the next few
weeks, Parallel experienced what must have felt like a million loud,
entitled Karens all asking to see the manager at the same time.

Most of these people knew perfectly well that Parallel's owner
was not a racist. They knew he wasn't trying to offend people with
the T-shirt. Some of them even knew that he hadn't sold the T-shirt
for a few months and that all the photographs being thrown around
were from years earlier.

But that didn't stop them.

When you're dealing with the woke, reality doesn't matter.

Eventually, major newspapers weighed in. *The Washington Post*
even ran a story titled "'Drunk Wives Matter' T-shirt pulled at
Virginia Restaurant amid uproar." The story quoted several online
liberal activists at their most sanctimonious and outraged. If you
were looking from the outside, you might have thought that the
whole world was up in arms about some stupid T-shirt that a wine
bar sold back in 2016. This small band of activists had succeeded

in turning something that absolutely no one should ever have cared about into a national news story.

But that wasn't the only cancel culture moment in Loudoun County. In December 2020, *The New York Times* ran a story about a white LCPS graduate who had her cheerleading scholarship pulled from the University of Tennessee because, years earlier as a 15-year old, she said in a Snapchat video after getting her learner's permit, "I can drive..." and ending the statement with a slang version of the N-word frequently used in music. A former friend acquired that deleted video, saved it for years, and then in the wake of the George Floyd riots used it to exact vengeance on the girl and cancel her with a social media campaign that resulted in her dream of cheerleading at an SEC school destroyed.

Of course, using that historically racist term is never acceptable. You wouldn't catch me ever saying it. But by the mid-2010s, that word had become so commonplace in pop culture and social media that it wasn't surprising that a 15-year-old who had never grown up in a world where that word was completely out-of-bounds in every context might not fully grasp how her mistake could be weaponized against her. What was surprising was the joy people had in resurfacing this ill-advised video to cancel her and get her scholarship revoked.

Needless to say, these two local incidents were very much on my mind when on March 12, 2021, I was invited to a meet and greet for Pete Snyder, a Republican candidate for governor. One of the people I had met recently was a local political leader in Loudoun County named Paul Chen, and he had asked me to attend the event at Parallel Wine Bar.

Wow! I thought. *Wasn't that the place that the woke mob tried to social media bomb out of existence? Made it so that anyone who went inside would be tarred and feathered and dragged through the streets while a real-life mob chanted accusations of racism at them?*

Given all that had occurred—the story in the *Post*, the thousands of tweets and Facebook posts—I wondered how or if the bar had recovered—especially during Covid.

Then I walked in.

A few minutes into the fundraiser, it became clear that everything was fine. Better than fine, in fact. The place was full, the wine and whiskey were flowing, and the small room in the back where Snyder was holding his event was filled with regular, good-natured people who all wanted to elect a candidate and have a good time. It certainly didn't appear that the online slander had had much impact, if any. The people behind those online attacks probably ran out of gas and moved to another target to cancel, and life went on at Parallel. Out in the real world, most people were normal, and they didn't give a damn about what went on in the private Facebook groups and Twitter feeds of woke activists.

Which brings me to an important lesson about cancel culture. As much as you might think that it's the end of the world, it's not. Real people in the real world—the ones who don't care what's on Twitter—will always have your back, especially when the people you're up against are joyless, mean-spirited bullies. Clearly, that's what happened with Parallel, whose customers showed up in droves as soon as the owner was being dangled over the flames by the mob.

Still, you can't always ignore it completely. Like it or not, we live in a world where the internet does occasionally creep into real life. And when that happens, your only choice is this: do not cower to the mob, do not bow to the mob, do not defend against the mob—flip the script and counterattack.

THE "ANTI-RACIST" PARENTS OF LOUDOUN COUNTY

During the meet and greet, I saw a guy named Scott, whom I'd spoken to a few times over the past few months. At first glance, Scott looked a little far out—like the kind of guy who had conspiracy theories about *other* conspiracy theories. He had a long goatee, and all he seemed to talk about was the corruption in Loudoun County. But once I got to know him, I realized that he was onto some pretty suspicious connections between the local NAACP and Loudoun County Public Schools. I also came to see that he was resourceful as hell and that his wife (a teacher in LCPS) and his two high school kids were all dedicated to his cause.

For most of the event, Scott and I talked about how things were going with his organization, Parents Against Critical Race Theory, or PACT. About a month earlier, I had helped him set up his organization as an LLC. We'd also spoken to a few other interested politicians who wanted to help parents push back against the school district, but nothing much had come of our efforts. At the time, I was seriously considering getting out of politics altogether to do something a little more lucrative, perhaps even returning to practicing law.

But sometimes, to paraphrase Michael Corleone in *The Godfather Part III*, just when you think you are out, they *pull* you back in.

While we were waiting for Snyder to speak, we started discussing a private Facebook group called "The Anti-Racist Parents of Loudoun County," which earlier in the day I had learned was creating a list of parents to be canceled for opposing critical race theory at Loudoun County Public Schools. At the time, there were a few thousand private Facebook groups for parents of all political stripes; most of them were just places for parents to coordinate afterschool activities and post articles they thought were interesting. But this sounded different.

I had actually learned about this group and its activities earlier that day. It had started when a member of the school board named Beth Barts asked for help to "push back against people in the community" who were opposed to critical race theory. Her post was clearly referring to Scott. In response to this post, people started posting names and pictures of anyone who'd ever associated with Scott. They referred to Patti Menders, another activist, as a "twatopuss."

Barts's post was inappropriate for an elected official, but in isolation it wasn't all that different from what you see on social media these days. Plus, Scott had been aggressively attacking her for months, and it looked from her post that this is what motivated her to post what she did.

But things got really nasty and out of hand when a woman told the members of the group that they needed to infiltrate other parents' groups that held different viewpoints, publicly expose them, send attack mailers, and hack their websites to either shut them down or redirect them to pro–critical race theory websites.[3] Everyone certainly seemed on board, and another woman suggested everyone go to her new post and start listing people by including their first and last names, area of residence, and school board representative.

Somehow, Scott had gotten the screenshots from the group, and several people had been listed before even the Snyder event had started. I suggested that the people who were listed write a letter to the United States Attorney for the Eastern District of Virginia as well as the Loudoun County Sheriff's Office. While saying nasty things about people in a private Facebook group is not a crime, the fact that a member called for people to hack others' websites could get law enforcement to look into whether some had engaged in solicitation to commit a federal cybercrime, and if the goal were to silence people, they could also investigate a conspiracy against rights.

Scott mentioned he was working with a reporter on a story about the group, and before I left, I told him to keep me posted and that I would help with the letter to law enforcement if he wanted to send one.

The following day, which was a Saturday, we were getting ready for our usual routine of hanging out with our friends and neighbors John and Christy. Neither was ideologically aligned with me, but they were also reasonable and could have political discussions without ending friendships. Just before they came over, the phone rang. It was Luke Rosiak from the *The Daily Wire*.

I had kept in touch with Luke since we first met for lunch a few months earlier after my story in *The Federalist*, and on this night he called me to be a sounding board for his latest story about Loudoun County: a private Facebook group with school board members, teachers, administrators and even the top county prosecutor was plotting against parents.

I told him I knew about some of it but didn't realize that so many government officials were in that group. He eventually mentioned to me that I had been one of the people listed in this group because of my earlier *Federalist* article. We finished up the conversation and I told him to keep me posted on the story but said I didn't want to go on the record because I didn't know enough details. Before I got off the phone, however, I asked him to send me the screenshot where I had been named.

About five minutes later, Luke sent me a screenshot of the post that mentioned me. There it was. The *Federalist* article. My name, my town, and my school board rep, along with some other commentary about how I was a mouthpiece in my community and how the person who posted it hoped I got "an eyeful." But what really got my attention was the identity of the person who put my name on there.

It was Ashley.

A neighbor, who I had once been friendly with, who had burned several neighborhood friendships during Covid and the George Floyd riots, had put my name on this list? Since I share the same last name as my two young daughters and my wife, she had effectively put their names on a list. With dozens of teachers and school administrators in that group. Now my kids' names were blacklisted, marked as problems, subject to cancellation because of a dad who wasn't sufficiently woke.

Wow!

Remember, this was on the heels of the attempt to destroy Parallel and the actual destruction of a young girl's cheerleading scholarship.

My first reaction was to walk over to Ashley's house, ring the doorbell, and have that face-to-face talk that she had never shown up for, but this time under much less friendly terms. But I knew that wouldn't do anything to stop her or her friends from their vicious attempts to cancel members of their community. Further, based on my previous experience dealing with her over the "horror" of my hanging a thin blue line flag, I figured she'd just hide and send her husband to clean up her messes so she could focus on creating new ones.

My second reaction was to close my eyes, take a few deep breaths, and think of a strategy. Mind unclouded, I realized that this was a moment where people would need to stand up to the bully. But I also knew that most of the people on that list probably wouldn't push back out of the very fear that this list-making exercise engendered. They didn't want to be canceled at their jobs, in the media, or with their friends. Even if they did want to shine a light on this, most of the people who were named in that group wouldn't have the political, legal, and public relationship experience or connections on how to execute it without making things much worse.

I just happened to be someone who knew exactly what to do and wasn't afraid to do it.

My mind then flashed to that scene in the movie *Taken* when Liam Neeson is on the phone with the bad guys right after he sees his daughter kidnapped: "What I do have are a particular set of skills. Skills I have acquired over a very long career. Skills that make me a nightmare for people like you."

It was at that moment that I decided to put my skills as a lawyer, a political communicator, and a student of history and strategy to use. I was going to stop these cancel culture commandos dead in their tracks. They wanted to publicly expose people? Good for them. I was going to flip the script and lead a counterattack where it would be WE who publicly exposed what they were planning before they could even get started executing those plans.

I thought about it for roughly 30 seconds more and said to myself, "I'm crossing the Rubicon." I called Luke Rosiak and told him I would talk to him on the record the next day.

When John and Christy came over, my plan had taken shape. I told them what I was going to do. I'd talk to *The Daily Wire*, I'd blow the story up, I would get myself on Tucker Carlson's show, and then I would write a new article in *The Federalist* explaining how writing my earlier article in *The Federalist* had gotten me placed on an enemies list.

They were supportive and thought that what Ashley and these others were doing was appalling. John commended me for not doing what he would have done, which was what I had initially wanted to do—walk over there and chew her out.

They were, however, skeptical if I could fully execute my plan as I had laid it out. My wife Elsie warned them that when I get off the couch and set my mind to something, it usually happens and it never works out well for the other side. My good friend Chris Pack would later put in in different terms: "Ian, you're basically John Wick. Except instead of killing your dog, they put you on an enemies list."

The next day, I told Luke the backstory that explained why a neighbor with whom I had once been friendly would put me on an enemies list. It was an important part of what I believed to be a larger story on how cancel culture had moved into the neighborhood level.

By Tuesday afternoon, the story had not yet posted, but I had looked at the full inventory of screenshots of the posting in the private Facebook group. I had wanted to put something out on Twitter after the story, but at the last minute, I changed my mind. I knew that *The Daily Wire* article would be serious and probably a bit dark, as it should be. But I wanted to add some levity to the moment. Again, a good counterattack means not going the traditional route, which, in this case, would be fighting fire with fire. I wanted to absorb the fire with a smile and a laugh while their attacks blew right back at them.

I decided to put out a snarky tweet including the screenshot of the post calling for hacking, public exposure, and infiltration next to the screenshot of Ashley adding my name and said: "Shot: Write op-ed in *The Federalist* questioning your local school district's commitment to critical race theory. Chaser: Watch your woke neighbor add your name to a targeting campaign that solicits illegal activities. Skipping her cookie party this year!"

Katie Pavlich, editor of Townhall.com, saw the tweet and ended up writing her own story on it, and by the time *The Daily Wire* story came out, the story was starting to get traction—at least on social media. I immediately pitched Fox News Primetime and Tucker Carlson. I had been on Fox News probably over 50 times discussing political campaigns and Department of Justice issues, including a few times on Tucker, but this was more than commentary. This was a personal story that could be delivered by a professional communicator.

Both shows wanted me to come on, but I ultimately had to go

for the biggest bang—Tucker. It was the highest-rated show, and this kind of story was right up his alley.

Tucker booked me for his show on St. Patrick's Day, and that morning I woke up, did a radio hit out of Chicago on the *Daily Wire* story, and started writing up that new op-ed I would submit to *The Federalist*. After spending the rest of my day doing my actual job consulting with clients on communications strategies, Fox News sent a car to pick me up around 6 p.m., and we pulled out for the hourlong drive from Loudoun County to Washington, D.C. As we were leaving, I saw our friend Jessica talking to Edna. I didn't think anything of it at the time, but Edna—and her middle finger—would soon enter the fight.

On my way to Tucker, a guy who I had recently met named Greg Stone texted me about the private Facebook group and jokingly labeled them "Chardonnay Antifa."

BOOM! That line would kill. When Greg gave me the okay to use it, I knew I had to work it in and stick the landing.

The Tucker hit was great, and when I dropped "Chardonnay Antifa," you could see him try to stifle a laugh. By Friday morning, the last tactic of the counterattack was complete. I had a new article in *The Federalist* titled "How Writing a Federalist Article Put Me on Chardonnay Antifa's Cancel List."

We had successfully launched a counterattack on these hateful, intolerant keyboard warriors in our community and had blown this story up beyond the wildest imaginations of the bad actors who thought they were untouchable. They had wanted to "infiltrate" and "publicly expose," but we had flipped the script on them, and now it was their hateful and scary actions that were publicly exposed.

Meanwhile, the Loudoun County Sheriff's Office was investigating Chardonnay Antifa in response to several police reports filed by others who had been on the list. With any luck, they would abandon their plans, reevaluate their tactics, and stop focusing on hating others.

But battle lines had been drawn, and a bigger war was on the horizon.

IDENTIFY THE "BAD GUYS" AND TAKE IT TO 'EM

KEY LESSON: Every conflict by its nature needs a good versus evil framework. But a neighbor versus neighbor fight on cancel culture will not have the kind of long-term implications that can make meaningful change. It is therefore important to find the right "bad guys" to fight. Equally as important, however, is to identify your strategy and not let distractions shift your focus.

"SILENCE IS COMPLICITY"

In the aftermath of my Tucker Carlson appearance, I waited. Sure, the texts and emails were rolling in from friends and supporters. Plenty of people had gotten a kick out of the "Chardonnay Antifa" line. But as far as I was concerned, that was the end of it. The goal was not to ruin the people who had taken part in the private Facebook group; it was to stop them and hold them accountable for what they had publicly planned to do.

But what about all those school board members who had been in the group? While only Beth Barts was directly involved in the incident at hand because of her initial post which led to the ensuing action by Chardonnay Antifa, five other school board members had been in the group and had engaged on school-related issues, viewable to 700 "anti-racist" parents in the community, to the exclusion of everyone else who sent their children to Loudoun County Public Schools.

Despite a week of being in the national news, Loudoun County Public Schools had said nothing about the controversy throughout the week.

After years in national politics, I had gotten used to the way big government organizations responded to exposés like the one I had just been a part of. There were meetings, press releases, and late-night phone calls to figure out how to proceed.

If I were a member of the Loudoun County School Board and I found out that some of my fellow board members were involved in a private social media group creating a list of parents to cancel, for instance, I would have been on the phone immediately to demand that they, at the very least, issue apologies, denounce the group's activities, and immediately get out of the group.

But in the aftermath, only one school board member had spoken up—Beth Barts, the school board member whose post kicked the whole thing off. And she was *not* backing down. On her Facebook page—which she had deftly used during her term to tick off her Democrat school board colleagues and conservative parents alike—Barts reposted with the following new message:

To be clear I will not apologize for advocating for the need to call out misinformation and the misrepresentation of our policies and plans to end systemic racism in our schools. I have and will continue to state loudly that LCPS is not teaching Critical Race Theory.

I did not call out any community members beyond the group that posted the images of me below two weeks ago and the resident who wrote a letter to the paper. I have no control over what others might have said in separate posts on social media.

I am proud to be both a parent and elected official who supports our Equity Statement and works hard to dismantle and reject racism. I will not ignore groups that attempt to silence me by calling me a liar as seen below.

The bottom two images were posted by PACT several weeks ago. A video about me is also available. It is hateful. While elected officials are fair game, we are allowed to defend ourselves from such attacks.

Silence is complicity. As an "anti-racist," I educate both myself and others on what Culturally Responsive Instruction is, I read to better understand what systemic racism does to our schools and I advocate for resources that allow our school system to level the playing field for marginalized communities. Most importantly I actively encourage others to do the same and will continue to do so.

I am clear in the post below and now in this post, that I represent myself only and not the board as a whole.

Sitting the parking lot of a Walgreens reading this after picking up a box of Fruity Pebbles (yes, I have a cereal addiction), I was taken aback. On one hand, she hadn't robustly denounced what her supporters did and how they interpreted her call to action. By not doing that, she was basically empowering them. On the other hand, I had just brought this entire episode into the national spotlight, and she did not cower or hide, like the rest of her colleagues on the school board who had said absolutely nothing publicly. One thing was clear to me about that statement—she had just made herself enemy number one to everyone that was angry about what had happened, and it seemed like she was willing to embrace the role.

At this time, I didn't really know much about any of the school board members, so I started some quick internet research on Barts. This wasn't the first time Barts had run into trouble on social media. She had been publicly reprimanded the previous November for sharing confidential school board information on Facebook[1], and the week before the Chardonnay Antifa incident, she had been formally censured by her own board for her activities on social media.[2]

At first, I was surprised that she didn't apologize for her involvement in the private Facebook group. But after learning about the situation, the more it started to make sense. She had seemingly found a way to anger the Democrats on the board and the more conservative-minded parents in the community. That meant that her only support was coming from the activist community that took her post as a call to action against parents who disagreed with the school board.

That put her in a tough position politically. Call out the activists who viewed her as a local hero and lose her last bit of support. Or largely give them a pass and hope it all went away. She chose the latter.

Still, I assumed that the rest of the school board would eventually do the right thing, denounce what had gone on in that group, apologize for being involved, and issue another censure or reprimand of Barts. It wouldn't make up for what happened, but it would certainly help rebuild the trust that they had lost.

It was only at 4:00 pm on the Friday of that week that Loudoun County Public Schools Interim Superintendent Scott Ziegler finally put out a statement addressing the issue. It came to my email as it did every parent in the county. And I couldn't believe what I was reading.

The statement was 12 paragraphs long and was primarily concerned with...clarifying "Rumors About LCPS Equity Work." Most of the statement was spin about how LCPS was not implementing critical race theory and any evidence to the contrary was a media distortion.

Then, buried in the 11th paragraph, I saw this:

> It has come to my attention that individuals, including some identifying themselves as LCPS employees, have made statements across social media about parents and their thoughts about the school division's equity work. LCPS recognizes the right of its employees to free speech, but does not condone anyone targeting members of the community for their viewpoint.

They were *identifying* themselves as LCPS employees. Are you kidding me? You had *six school board members* in there with a host of other teachers and administrators. I was born at night, but I wasn't born last night.

Before this response came, I was content to have played a role in stopping Chardonnay Antifa from continuing to try to cancel people and businesses in Loudoun County. But sitting there on March 19, 2021, I realized that there was something more nefarious happening than one outspoken school board member and a few repressed, angry white leftist keyboard warriors.

The school board was too interested in protecting their own to do anything to fix the situation. The public was rightfully outraged. Parents were demanding to know what their children were learning in schools, and they were fed up with the nonsense they had seen during the lockdowns. My group chat was blowing up with explicit images of schoolbooks about five-year-olds changing genders, insane lessons built on critical race theory, and teacher trainings calling thin people "oppressors."

I had gone on the most-watched cable news show in the world to draw attention to this issue on my own, but it barely made a dent. The school board seemed oblivious to the fact that they stood at the precipice of their own doom.

For the rest of the night, I walked around in a state of deep thought. I tried constantly to come up with more ideas. Was writing more op-eds the answer? Was it trying to meet with more journalists to get the story out? Whatever happened, I knew one thing: something was going to have to be done.

THE BAD GUYS

We were mad at wokeness.

We were mad at our neighbors.

We were mad at teachers, public officials, and everyone who had ever told us we were crazy to be concerned about what our children were learning in school.

But none of that would matter unless we could answer two simple questions. First: Who was really doing this? Second: How could we stop them?

I've noticed in these local political fights that people tend to lash out in every direction without a very targeted and specific plan of attack.

Rather, you need to do what the left has done so well and as was laid out in Saul Alinsky's *Rules for Radicals*. Pick the target, freeze it, personalize it, and polarize it. Or, as I like to call it, find the bad guys, attack the bad guys.

When you're in a political battle with your public school system, your only target is the school board and the senior staff. The members, working with the superintendent and his or her staff, make policy, hire and fire teachers and staff, and are charged with representing the will of the people. But all across the country, they are not doing that. Instead, they are focused on all the wrong priorities. This certainly isn't just something germane to Loudoun County—this applies to your school board as well.

This is not to say the other political allies, influential special interest groups, and woke keyboard warriors are not important in the grand scheme of things. But if they don't have an official apparatus to influence—the school board and the superintendent—then they have limited power. Which is why elected school board representatives and the people they hire to implement policies and run the schools should always be the focus.

Therefore, it's important to know what motivates your school board member. You will generally find four types of people on the school board: (1) political climbers, (2) radical activists, (3) people who actually care about public service, and (4) people who actually care about public service but have been swayed, deceived, and eventually neutered by those in the first two categories.

In Loudoun County, there are nine school board members. The way it was composed in 2021, I would say that there were at least three political climbers: Democrats Atoosa Reaser and Ian Serotkin and Republican John Beatty. Brenda Sheridan, who was chairwoman at the time, was your textbook radical activist. Four more fell into the category of well-intentioned people who had been beaten down by the radical activist and political climbers. Then there was Beth Barts, who seemed like she was a radical activist but, as we will see later, may have been far savvier than her colleagues or I gave her credit for.

Is this something I had figured out by March 2021? No, it would take me months to understand those dynamics. But I did know in March 2021 that if change was going to be made, it was going to have to focus on this: six members of the Loudoun County School Board were part of a private Facebook group that tried to cancel parents for speaking out against LCPS policies, practices, and conduct. When this was exposed, they did not apologize to the parents targeted or use their platform as elected officials to denounce the group. Three of them would stay in the group for another five months, with the rest gradually leaving during that time. If they weren't going to hold themselves accountable, then we, their constituents, would do it, and we would not distract ourselves with any other opponents.

The only question was how. School board elections were not until November 2023—two and a half years away. That's a long time to send your children to a school system that is trending woke.

As it happened, I had just taken on a client in California who was locked in a battle with his local Board of Supervisors over some Covid-related policies. Working with them, I learned that you could "recall" elected officials, although every state had different mechanisms for doing so. What if we did that here?

I went to the Virginia Code and started reading. It turned out that Virginia did have a process for removing local officials, although that process was among the most complicated in the nation. According to the removal provision, we needed to begin by collecting signatures from enough people to equal 10 percent of the people who'd voted in the last election. Then, once we had the signatures, we could go to court, where a judge would decide if the officials in question were guilty of "neglect of duty, misuse of office, or incompetence in the performance of his or her duty." But to make matters more complicated, once the citizens submitted the petition, it was the responsibility of the Commonwealth Attorney in the county to prosecute what was a *quasi-civil and quasi-criminal* case. And remember, that Commonwealth Attorney had ridden to power on almost $1 million from George Soros. Even worse, she herself had been part of the Anti-Racist Parents of Loudoun County Facebook group.

Regardless, I knew that we had a case that six school board members had neglected their duty or shown incompetence in the performance of their duties. I hadn't figured out the case just yet, but that would come. I did know that I needed to get over 17,000 people to agree with me by signing a petition. Then we would deal with the Soros-backed prosecutor later.

It turned out that for most of the elections that had given us these particular members of the school board, somewhere between 10,000 and 20,000 people had turned out to vote. Of course, I didn't know more than a handful of them at that time, and I certainly wasn't one of them, either. As is often the case with local elections, only the most dedicated partisans show up to the polls, which means that the people who get elected are often wildly to one side or the other of the political aisle.

But the low turnout was good news for me. Since we only needed signatures equal to 10 percent of the total votes cast for the last election, we would only need around 1,000 to 2,000 signatures to file in court.

That Saturday night, once again with our friends John and Christy over, I explained my idea.

Christy then said, "What if you don't get the signatures?" Honestly, I didn't know the answer but responded, "I'll figure it out." She followed up by asking, "What if you lose in court?"

It was a fair question. What if we put in all this effort only to lose at the end? But it misses something crucial that is important for everyone to recognize—when you are fighting a political battle with your local government, individual wins are certainly preferable, but the key is the fight. The more people join the cause, the more the politics of your town, county, or state will have to react. If you create enough of a storm and get a strong enough reaction, you will create change and you will win.

In this case, Virginia was in the middle of the only real competitive governor's race in the country. Terry McAuliffe, the former Democratic governor, would be facing a serious challenge from either private equity veteran Glenn Youngkin or entrepreneur Pete Snyder. From speaking with people around town, I knew there was a great deal of excitement for both candidates.

If we could tie our fight to the national attention that Virginia was getting because of this governor's race, we would win either way. Hell, I thought, maybe this could be the issue that tipped the scales for one candidate or another.

I explained this to Christy and replied, "If this plays out as an issue the way that I think it will, even if we lose, we win. Hell, it may even have an impact in the statewide elections this November."

Turns out, that was an understatement.

PICK THE RIGHT STRATEGY

First, never confuse tactics with strategy. As Sun Tzu said in *The Art of War*, "Strategy without tactics is the slowest route to victory. Tactics without strategy is the noise before defeat." Strategy defines your long-term goal and the overarching plan on how to reach that goal. Tactics, on the other hand, are concrete steps along the way that fit within the overall strategy.

Utilizing the recall procedure is not a strategy, it is a tactic. The strategy was to use that tactic to bring attention to what was wrong with the Loudoun County School Board and administration. This would serve to bring about a new coalition of parents who would become a new force to be reckoned with and could no longer be ignored while well-funded unions and special interests used their power to monopolize the policy-making duties of those who were elected to serve parents and students. Tactically, the very act of gathering thousands of signatures would help awaken parents and create enthusiasm, momentum, and hope for change. This, then, would be a key tactic to help implement the strategy.

A huge concern of mine was to make sure that the reasons behind the removal tactic were sufficiently broad to create a coalition that included Republicans, Independents, and Democrats. Yet, to create that broad coalition, the reasons for removal must be targeted, easy to understand, and about conduct, not policy.

There were certainly significant issues that could be the centerpiece of our strategy, implemented in part through the removal tactic. Schools had been closed for a year, and parents had been fighting to reopen them ever since. Critical race theory was another issue that had galvanized parents enough to lead to the creation of an enemies list in plain sight of six school board members. But there were two problems with those issues. First, they both related to policy decisions, and we would have virtually no chance of getting a judge to remove a sitting school board member for a policy decision, however bad it might be. Secondly, there may be people who hadn't come around to schools reopening or thought that critical race theory was just a far-right buzzword.

Fortunately, the answer was staring me right in the face.

Thinking back to the private Facebook group, I came up with a legal theory that had no precedent either way but would be a novel claim that a court would have to address. With six out of nine school board members present in the private Facebook group, it constituted a quorum per Virginia's Freedom of Information Act—that would make it a meeting that would have required notice, public access, and minutes. None of that had happened, making it a FOIA violation.

But the school board members' presence in the Facebook group could also be a violation of the First Amendment. Only those with a properly woke viewpoint could attend this digital meeting. Further, any comments by a school board member in the group would only be inviting replies from members of the group. This effectively shut out all but 600 to 700 people from commenting on a government official's Facebook post. A recent case in Loudoun County (*Davison v. Randall*) had made it clear that such behavior was unconstitutional.

Finally, the school board's own code of conduct required members to "welcome and encourage active cooperation by Loudoun County residents…with respect to establishing policy on current school operation" and "to strive step by step toward ideal conditions for most effective board service to my community, in a spirit of teamwork and devotion to public education as the greatest instrument for the preservation of perpetuation of our representative democracy."[3]

With that in mind, our strategy would be to build a coalition of parents by raising awareness of how the Loudoun County School Board violated state FOIA law, the First Amendment, and its own code of conduct when it stood by and did nothing as radical activists plotted against parents who were on the wrong side of the school board's politics. The removal petitions would be drafted solely along those lines, and we would not stray from that key message.

Now I had a strategy, a key tactic, and the messaging that would serve as our mission statement and guide us to success. I just needed to operationalize and implement it. For that, I would need a team.

My first step was to set up a meeting with those people with whom I had connected during the pond renaming incident—my neighbors Jessica, Beth, Darris, and Stacy. Jessica offered to host a meeting on her back deck and also suggested that I reach out to the moms who were part of a Facebook group called LCPS Can Do Better, which was fighting to open schools. I did that and invited Kay Greenwell and Cheryl Onderchain to the meeting. My final call was to Paul Chen, who was more plugged into the local political scene than the rest of us and could help us push this into the local political ecosystem.

We all met at Jessica's house. Many of us had never met beyond social media correspondence, email, or phone. But we got to business pretty quickly. I pitched my idea on the strategy and the removal procedure and explained my legal theories and the detailed the requirements to get to court.

It certainly didn't take long for the team to get on board. They were sick of a school board that was keeping schools closed, was violating its own code of conduct, and was demonstrating to the county that it was irresponsible and unqualified to represent an engaged community.

There was some talk of removing just Beth Barts, the whole board or adding the seventh Democrat to the list, but the strategy required only targeting the six who were in the private Facebook group: Brenda Sheridan, Atoosa Reaser, Barts, Ian Serotkin, Denise Corbo, and Leslee King. Yes, they were all Democrats. That meant that the three who weren't part of the group—Republicans Jeff Morse and John Beatty and Democrat Harris Mahedavi— were off the list.

Once the decision was made to go, we planned out the announcement. We would call ourselves "Loudoun Parents for Education" and hold a press conference outside the next school board meeting announcing the recall campaign.

With only two days to prepare, we moved quickly. Several of us decided to give remarks at the press conference about why we were taking action. Paul, Cheryl, Jessica, Darris, and I would speak, so each of us worked on remarks to give at a podium with the press covering it. In case the press didn't show, which is always a possibility, Stacy and her husband had planned out the logistics of how to livestream the press conference on Facebook. Meanwhile, Beth quickly ordered signs that said "Loudoun Parents for Education" that people could hold up behind speakers to show the appearance of an organized group. Meanwhile, Cheryl and Kay reached out to their large network to get a group of 20 people to stand behind the speakers holding the signs.

The morning of the event, I drafted a press release and a media advisory to send to local and national media. The release was short and concise but clearly communicated what we were doing (starting a campaign to remove six school board members), why we were doing it (the school board members violated FOIA, the First Amendment, and their own code of conduct), and how we would do it (by spending the next several months gathering signatures). The release would go out *after* the press conference, but the advisory would go out a few hours before and simply give the time and place of the press conference as well as a vague description of what it was about—addressing the private Facebook group.

The week before, I had put together a press list of local news outlets simply by going to their websites and collecting reporter and news desk email addresses along with the email addresses of national reporters who had been covering school issues. This isn't as complicated as it seems—it really just takes a few hours of online research into who is covering school closures, union pressure on schools, and woke ideology in schools. Usually, you can get the emails right from the reporters' bylines.

By the time I was ready to send the advisory, I had a solid list of 150 emails that included all the targeted media outlets as well as friends and former colleagues who might help spread the word. Once I sent it, Stacy and I called through the local outlets to make sure that they saw the advisory and would attend. This is always good practice—it helps drive the press to events that they might have missed because of an influx of emails that they receive every day.

The hour came, and we held our press conference with about 20 people behind a podium with our "Loudoun Parents for Education" signs. Most of the local news outlets showed up, and Stacy successfully set up a livestream to push on our new Facebook page, which we had made the day before.

The speeches were all great, but more important was the visual of two dozen parents holding a press conference to announce that they would be recalling six members of the school board. Immediately after, I jumped in my car to call in for a radio hit with Larry O'Connor of WMAL. It would be the first of many appearances on his show, one that reached the beltway crowd but did not shy away from covering important local issues.

After the radio hit, I hopped in a car to get to Fox News for my TV appearance. I watched the public comment portion of the meeting on my phone, and speaker after speaker was lighting into the school board for their participation in the Anti-Racist Parents of Loudoun County group. Even the quiet, conservative member John Beatty spoke out against his colleagues. But none of it seemed to matter. There were no statements from any of the offending board members about what had happened. Not a single word.

I did my Fox hit, and host Brian Kilmeade hit the nail on the head when he said—as he would say multiple other times throughout the summer and fall—"they messed with the wrong dad."

If for no other reason, that line meant the world to me. My daughters would always know I would fight like hell for them, no matter the odds.

Soon the country would learn that Loudoun County was filled with moms and dads just as motivated as me.

TURN YOUR FIGHT INTO MUST-SEE TV

KEY LESSON: You cannot inspire in the darkness; you cannot pressure the enemy without the pressure of bad publicity. The greatest generals in history always knew that there must be an element of showmanship to the battle.

KEEP IT SIMPLE

So we had the makings of an organization. We knew that if we were going to have any hope of succeeding, we'd need a whole lot of volunteers who were willing to go door-to-door or sit in parking lots in 90-degree weather asking people to sign our petition. We would also need money for lawyers to bring the removal cases to court and maybe even to hire people to collect signatures depending on whether we would be able to get enough volunteers.

But before we could raise money or attract volunteers, we needed to build an actual organization that could develop a brand and execute our strategy.

When you're working with the media, a good name can make

or break you, so I had a call with my friends Gerrit Lansing and Jordan Gehrke to talk it out.

What, we wondered, was a name that parents could get behind? What was the name that they would want to say 10,000 times while they knocked on doors and tried to fight for their children? I suggested we go with something generic sounding, like sticking with "Loudoun Parents for Education." Gerrit and Jordan thought we needed something stronger and suggested "Fight for Families," "Fight for Students," and "Fight for Schools."

In the end, we decided that the simplest name was probably the best. We wanted to leave no doubt in anyone's minds what we stood for—and what we fought for.

So the organization "Fight for Schools" was born.

In the following weeks, I worked to fully operationalize the organization that would carry out the strategy. This can seem like grunt work, but it's very important if you want your movement to grow. In addition to your main tactical goal—collecting signatures and getting rid of six incompetent and morally weak members of the school board, in our case—you'll want to raise money and plan for future operations as well. That way, the movement doesn't end when you've done the small task you set out to do. Things can keep growing, and you can make change on a national level.

When you're setting up a political organization, the first step is to decide what kind of entity you want to be. A 501(c)(3)—named for the portion of the federal tax code—is a charitable organization that can engage in activity designed to benefit the public welfare—think the ACLU before they stopped operating on principles and became nothing more than a tool of the woke left. A 501(c)(3) can accept donations that aren't public and are tax-deductible for the donor. But it comes with lots of compliance costs and can't engage in electioneering—in other words, you can't spend money to elect or defeat a candidate for office.

There was also the option of a 501(c)(4), named for another section of the federal tax code. Again, donations are anonymous, but they are not tax-deductible. With this kind of organization, you can engage in electioneering, but it can only account for 49 percent of total activity. The remaining 51 percent has to be dedicated to advocacy. So, in practice, you could spend a little less than half of your money and resources airing ads about how one candidate was terrible and the other one wasn't, while the rest of the time you could only push for policy changes.

There was a lot of benefit to filing as a 501(c)(4). We would be spending far more of our resources on advocacy and the legal process of removing school board members. Further, donations would be anonymous, so Chardonnay Antifa couldn't fire up their angry social media mob of crazy white ladies to attack donors and try to get them fired.

But ultimately, we decided on a Super PAC under Virginia law. Donations would be public, but we would have the flexibility to spend on whatever we wanted. This also meant that people would see all expenditures, which meant no one would get paid. I thought that this would create a level of transparency that would prevent people from calling us a "dark money" group that was doing this just to make money. Both of those things were absolutely true, but that didn't stop the media and Loudoun's leftist cartel from constantly lying about it!

Once we decided on the organization type, we had to incorporate with the Commonwealth of Virginia and file with the state board of elections. We also needed to draft bylaws, get at least three board members, and elect corporate officers. Add in a website, an email list, social media accounts, and finally a donation platform that would allow us to accept donations, and we would be off and running.

Luckily, I had some help from my days at the National Republican Congressional Committee. A few friends at the law firm Holtzman Vogel helped me get the whole Fight for Schools operation up and running. But if you don't have the contacts, don't worry. Send an email to info@fightforschools.com and we can connect you with someone who can help you through the process.

Within days, we were incorporated and filed with the Virginia Board of Elections as a Super PAC. Stacy helped me design a website and set up some social media accounts, and I brought on Crosby Ottenhoff as our political accounting/compliance company to open a bank account, handle our accounting, and file the financial reports that were required to be submitted to the board of elections each quarter. We also used Gerrit's company REVV for our donation platform to accept donations. This way we wouldn't have to be worried about getting shut down by GoFundMe or some other platform that could easily be pressured by left-wing activists. I was the president, and we had Jessica, Stacy, Kay, Paul, Beth, and Cheryl as our directors.

We were ready to go. Now it was time to tell the world.

In mid-April, I pressed play on the website and pitched the exclusive story of our launch to Fox News. The people at Fox had been friendly to our mission in the past, and I had a feeling they'd be interested in covering the story. Luckily, I was right. But I'll admit that I was lucky. After a few years in politics, I had the contacts and a little inside knowledge about how to get myself and my organization on the big television networks. Here, in case you're wondering, is all the knowledge about getting on TV that I've gained from my 11 long years in American politics:

1. Build contacts in the media. Take them to get lunch or coffee and get to know what kind of stories they are interested in. Even if the reporter is not from a "friendly" outlet, it's still important to build relationships. You may not always get the coverage you want from some of these media outlets, but if you have developed a good enough relationship, the reporter will at least include a comment and will be less likely to completely screw you in a story.

2. Give exclusives to reporters who you know will be the fairest with your story. That means that whatever you are pitching them, they get to publish it first before you send it to any other reporter or in a press release.

3. Always make your exclusive pitches off the record and define your terms. For example, tell the reporter that the pitch is off the record, show them your release, and let them know that if they are interested, they can run it as an exclusive no earlier than a certain time. If they accept those terms, then you really shouldn't share with anyone else until their story runs. Once it does, send your release to everyone else and use social media to push their story.

4. Pay a subscription fee for an email service, like Campaign Monitor or MailChimp. Do the legwork to look up local reporter email addresses as well as the emails of national reporters who are clearly interested in the issues

that you are working on. Also make sure to include in your email list other local and national influencers who have a good social media following. Design a template for press releases and send them in the same format every time. The template should have a "subscribe" button to allow new people to sign up for your emails, and you'll need to follow the instructions to create a sign-up form for your emails on your website as well. When we started Fight for Schools, I was able to build on my email list and get to around 700 people who were friends, family, and reporters I either knew or had added because I knew they would be interested in the issues. That list organically grew to over 20,000 in a little over a year.

Remember: Just because you're not on Tucker Carlson's show minutes after your launch doesn't mean it was a failure. There are plenty of local television stations and newspapers who are always looking for stories, too. If you can get exposure there, the bigger outlets might notice if enough people share your story on social media.

In our case, the Fox News story helped quite a bit. The story, written by a reporter named Sam Dorman, got out all the information we wanted our audience to have. It named the six school board members we wanted to unseat, told people how to donate, and quoted me at length about the problems.[1]

Which brings me to another point. When you're getting interviewed by a reporter—no matter what side they're on—make sure you know exactly what you want to say in advance. Spend a few minutes jotting down the points you'd like to hit for your quote, and make sure to tell a compelling story. That'll ensure that the reporter uses your whole quote rather than breaking it up into sound bites.

Here, for instance, is what I said to Sam Dorman when he interviewed us about our launch.

> For the sake of our children, Loudoun County parents cannot wait until 2023 to elect new leaders. Fortunately, Virginia law provides a remedy for new elections; recalling government officials that have abused their office or been incompetent in the performance of their duties. Both apply here, whether applied to the school board's failure to reopen schools, its implementation of dangerously divisive critical race theory, and its active or passive participation in tactics designed to intimidate students, parents and teachers from exercising their First Amendment rights.

Now, I'm not saying this is a perfect quote, but it does do a few things right. First, it's not broken up into a bunch of little sentences. Second, it follows a train of logic and argument. And finally, it mentions the issues that I had learned were the most important to parents all over the country. The goal was to have parents and concerned citizens read about "divisive critical race theory, and its active or passive participation tactics designed to intimidate students" and feel a flash of recognition. Luckily, the story about our launch ended up using the full quote uninterrupted.

When they story came out, it hit like a thunderclap. We received messages across the country supporting what we were doing and thanking us for standing up. Of course, Chardonnay Antifa had a field day with it on the local social media channels. A local middle school teacher predictably said on Facebook that we were "putting our racism on full display."

The publicity was great for our bank account. In the first day after the story went up, we raised close to $7,000 in online donations alone. These were people who'd seen the story, followed the link, and donated a few dollars to support our cause. For a moment, I marveled at how amazing it was that we'd gotten that much money already. The next day, I promoted the story with a few radio and television interviews, which helped push online donations close to $15,000.

In the days to come, that number would keep growing.

Now, of course, all we had to do was figure out a way to collect more than 17,000 signatures from people in our neighborhoods.

But a funny thing happened while we were building out that plan—we started a movement!

TAKE CENTER STAGE

During the second act of the movie *Gladiator*, Russell Crowe's character Maximus yells in frustration to lackadaisical spectators after he had won another battle as a gladiator: "Are you not entertained?"

Several scenes later, Oliver Reed's character Proximo, an old gladiator turned promoter, gives Maximus a lesson to succeed in the big-league gladiatorial games of the Colosseum: "Listen to me. Learn from me. I was not the best because I killed quickly. I was the best because the crowd loved me." Later, Proximo added, "Win the crowd and you will win your freedom."

After formally launching Fight for Schools, much of what we were doing was earned media. The media was focused on critical race theory in schools, and while that wasn't why we were seeking to remove school board members, it was the plotted cancellation of opponents of critical race theory that gave rise to this whole effort. As long as we could walk and chew gum at the same time by staying on message when it came to the specific reasons for the removal campaigns, there was no harm in inserting ourselves into the public debate about critical race theory.

Of course, Loudoun County Public Schools made it easier to thread that needle because they kept denying that it was "teaching critical race theory." This was technically true—it wasn't teaching a course by that name, but it was adopting the concepts of critical race theory in its teacher training and classroom instruction.

Now that we were on the map, people in the community started sending us evidence demonstrating clearly that Loudoun County Public Schools was all in on critical race theory. One video showed a teacher berating a student for refusing to recognize the race of two people in a picture. According to the teacher, the student was wrong for not looking at people through the lens of race as opposed to using a color-blind approach. That video ended up getting over 250,000 views, largely thanks to our expanding email list and ability to move things to national, right-of-center media that would write about these issues. And every time we sent out a piece of information like that, the email list grew and grew and grew. It also added to our strategic message that the school board was not being transparent to the community.

During this time in April, the media outlets started having other parents on beyond just me. I still did the bigger hits, but it was gratifying to see Paul and Cheryl out doing *Fox and Friends* and representing Fight for Schools. With more parents out talking, people were going to start to understand that this was not some Washington, D.C., operation; rather, it was a true grassroots movement. Heck, one of the favorites for the Republican nomination for governor, Pete Snyder, started name-dropping us on the radio and even asked for my endorsement! I was more than happy to do it because I knew he understood what was happening on the ground. I didn't quite get that sense from the other favorite, Glenn Youngkin. At that time, he seemed more safe, traditional, and cautious of the growing movement in Loudoun. That said, my endorsing Pete ruffled a few feathers, but at that point I had built up enough of a reputation as a fighter; no one was going to disown me for it!

I also took this time to really build out the case against Loudoun County Public Schools. Through the Freedom of Information Act, I found an invoice from the Equity Collaborative for training teachers in critical race theory. I dug up the slide deck the Collaborative used for that training. One page said that Western liberalism, meritocracy, and equal opportunity perpetuate systemic racism.

Well, when all the people on the left were trying to claim that critical race theory was just a law school class and that the non-elite couldn't even define it, I just gained a new weapon. Here it is, right in Loudoun County Public Schools material! Oh, and when you ask me to define it, I'm going to use the definition gifted to us but the Equity Collaborative: "Western liberalism, meritocracy, and equal opportunity perpetuate systemic racism."

The first chance to fire off that information was right at the Loudoun County School Board's public comment on April 27. This would be my first time speaking at a school board meeting since the previous October and the first time confronting the board after spending the past month blasting them in national media and launching a political action committee that would try to legally remove them from their positions.

To really spin them around, I wore a Jackie Robinson "42" T-shirt and asked the board how it liked the spotlight of accountability. Then I pointed out that the Equity Collaborative was still charging it $650 per hour and that one of its sessions was about critical race theory training, which included the line about Western liberalism, meritocracy, and equal opportunity perpetuating systemic racism.

I closed the speech with a line that would become a rallying cry for Fight for Schools: "We have more tips than you have time, but we can do this all day, every day."

It was a riff off Captain America's line from the Marvel movies: "I can do this all day." As you can see already, me ripping lines from my favorite movies would become a recurring theme in this fight. It was fun for me, but it did connect to what I was trying to do—for those who understood the reference, I was just a normal guy watching the same movies as millions of dads with their kids, even if they knew nothing about our fight with the school board. They were also great, punchy, entertaining lines that served to inspire and capture the imagination of those watching and listening, which was fully part of our mission. Again, we weren't there to provide entertainment, but the reality of life is that three-second sound bites can go a long way toward getting the kind of attention you need to grow the movement.

In addition to me, speaker after speaker ripped the school board for its critical race theory push. It should have been clear to the school board by this point that those parents weren't going anywhere. They weren't going to be lied to, they weren't going to be bullied by activists lined up with the school board, and they would keep sending FOIA requests and bringing the heat at school board meetings.

The problem at this point was that, while we were building our brand and building our coalition of supporters, we weren't doing what we had announced. We had made no move to start the process of gathering signatures to remove those six school board members. I had spoken to some acquaintances who were running the organization that was financially supporting the Fairfax recall efforts. They told me that they were spending $100,000 to hire people to gather signatures. We had increased our money raised to about $25,000 at the time, but I thought I would have to raise a whole lot more money to be able to collect the requisite amount of signatures.

I kept delaying, thinking to myself that a solution to the problem of how to start getting signatures would magically pop into my brain while going for a run or taking a shower.

That's pretty much exactly what happened.

The Virginia Republican Convention on May 8, 2021, was going to be a drive-through operation at the VAGOP 10th District Headquarters in Loudoun. That meant there would be thousands of Republicans going to vote at this convention for their choice for governor, lieutenant governor, and attorney general. If I set up a signing booth with volunteers on the way out, we could make a major dent in the number of signatures we needed!

I made some calls. Stacy and Patti Menders, head of the Loudoun County Republican Women's Club, helped get me volunteers to work on that Saturday. Geary Higgins, 10th District

Chair, gave me permission to set up the signatures station in the parking lot where people would drive out after having voted. We were good to go—except we didn't even have petitions.

Fortunately, another resident named Austin Levine had launched a Recall Beth Barts campaign that January. It never went anywhere, but he did have a lawyer who had been getting petitions drafted. As it turned out, that lawyer also worked at Holtzman Vogel, which was the firm that had set up Fight for Schools. We were able to get all six petitions turned around and ready to launch on that Saturday.

It was a crazy weather day, changing from sun to rain to hail to wind and back around the roller coaster again. It was also very much trial by fire. At first, we thought only a person who lived in a school board member's district could sign to remove them. We determined that wasn't true after an hour. We also didn't have a system for determining which school board member a resident could sign for—everyone could sign for the at-large member, Denise Corbo, but for the rest, only people who lived in the school board member's district could sign.

Then we also had a typo on Ian Serotkin's petition, which referred to him as a "she" throughout. This was annoying but also somewhat ironic. Given our leftist school board's obsessions with gender being fluid, would Serotkin really fight a few signatures in court because the pronoun was wrong?

In any event, it was a wildly successful day. We collected well over 1,500 signatures and had learned on the fly what we would need to do to be more efficient and make sure that everyone was signing for the right school board member. Sure, we could have been more buttoned up on the technical requirements of who could witness signatures from which district, but the fact was that this process was so rare and so frequently unsuccessful, there wasn't a whole lot of information out there. Ultimately, we figured it out through experience and always operating out of an abundance of caution and doing more than what we thought was required.

We also now had volunteers and a community that was aware that these petitions were out there to be signed. This resulted in a massive outreach effort to either volunteer or sign the petition. In other words, we needed to scale up.

That is how the Army of Moms was formed.

THE ARMY OF MOMS

It didn't happen all at once. But it started on May 8. It was a core team of moms in their 30s and 40s who were smart, educated, hilarious, frustrated with Loudoun County Public Schools, and ready to fight like hell for their children.

Amy Jahr. Erin Dunbar. Sandra Vaughn. Jessica Mendez. Michael Primazon. Erin Brown. Emily Curtis. Stacy Markus. Beth Hess. Elicia Brand. Suzanne Satterfield. Jamie Fortier. Laura Johnson. Michele Mege. Kate O'Hara. Ronda Nassib. Kay Greenwell. Cheryl Onderchain. Erin Smith. Emily Emschwiller. Patti Menders. Carri Michon. Abbie Platt. Emily Borkholder. Anne Miller. Debbie Edsall. Shelly Shlebrch. Karlee Copeland. Shawntel Cooper. And Elizabeth Perrin.

This core group would be responsible for collecting thousands of signatures, delivering devastatingly effective school board speeches, hosting events and parties, and being the tip of the spear of this national parents' revolution.

By the end of May, this Army of Moms would get a chance to flex its muscles, become a powerful force, and give rise to another buzzworthy term that only added to the real-life movie we were broadcasting to the country.

But before that happened, the biweekly school board meetings started becoming must-see television. On May 8, a group of parents, most of whom I didn't know at the time, had posters made up with pages from some of the near-pornographic books that 14-year-old girls had been assigned. They went one after the other, reading uncomfortable sexualized language to the school board as part of their speeches. It got covered for days, with new parents like Elizabeth Perrin, Joe Mobley, and Elicia Brand going on Fox News and becoming overnight stars. It was a well-executed earned media tactic, and it upped the game with the Loudoun County School Board.

But the most newsworthy item that day wasn't planned—well, it wasn't planned by anyone I knew. Rather, a Black woman named Shawntel Cooper had spoken with Elizabeth at the drive-through convention. Shawntel decided to come to the school board and give a speech, which was a passionate deconstruction of critical race theory from the perspective of a conservative Black woman with two biracial children.

In her speech, she said: "In the words of Martin Luther King, Jr. 'I have a dream' that my four little children will one day live in a nation where they will not be judged by the color of their skin. But by the content of their character. Now I have a dream that we will implement love, not hate. Or supporting another Jim Crow agenda. CRT is not an honest dialogue; it is a tactic that was used by Hitler and the Ku Klux Klan on slaves very many years ago to dumb down my ancestors so we could not think for ourselves. CRT is racist, it is abusive, it discriminates against one's color. Let me educate you: an honest dialogue does not oppress, an honest dialogue does not admit hatred or injustice, it is to communicate without deceiving people. Today we don't need your agreement, we want action and a backbone for what we ask for today, to ban CRT. We don't want your political advertisement to divide our children or belittle them. Think twice before you indoctrinate such racist theories. You cannot tell me what is or is not racist. Look. At. Me. I had to come down here to tell you to your face that we are coming together, and we are strong. This will not be the last greet and meet, respectfully."

I was in the hallway waiting to speak when I heard her speech—I was floored. If I could publicize this one-minute clip, Loudoun County would be all over the news. I asked a friend to clip the raw video and send it my way. In the meantime, I went in to give my speech and added a line after hearing Shawntel speak: "Loudoun County is ground zero in the fight against critical race theory." I was half right. It was ground zero, but critical race theory would be only one component of a broader fight that would soon take shape.

That evening, I tweeted the raw video of Shawntel Cooper's speech and then sent out my tweet via email to my now-massive email list. It was the first thing I ever put on social media that legitimately went viral. Within a few days, that tweet received 4 million impressions. It generated dozens of stories about her speech and appearances by Shawntel on Tucker Carlson and Sean Hannity. It really seemed to supercharge the story of Loudoun but also the courage of people to start showing up to school board meetings, getting involved with Fight for Schools, and starting their own pop-up events or door-knocking for signatures to recall the school board.

A quick pointer on the mechanics of making a video go viral, which my friend Zack Roday had told me a few weeks before. DO NOT TWEET YOUTUBE OR RUMBLE CLIPS! Doing so requires people to click through the video and doesn't present as well on Twitter as simply saving a one-minute clip and tweeting it directly. This was the first time I put that advice to use, and boy did it work.

Shawntel's speech was the first viral speech, but it would not be the last.

And we wouldn't have to wait long.

DO NOT GET STUCK IN THE MUD

KEY LESSON: Always be in motion. The opposition, however clumsily, will start to fight back and try to engage you on their terms. Do not fall into the trap. When they zig, you must zag and keep moving forward to your goal.

BOILING POINTS

When it comes to injustice, everyone has a boiling point. For some parents in our community, that boiling point was pretty low, and thank God it was. Without them, we might not have a movement today.

Almost as soon as the schools first locked down for Covid, these parents could tell that something had changed. Parents had barely been consulted before this decision was made, and their protests went largely unanswered by the school board.

It was a sign of things to come.

My own boiling point came when I learned I was on Chardonnay Antifa's "enemies list," although there had been previous incidents that raised my temperature slightly.

For a lot of people in the community, the boiling point came as soon as they found out about Policy 8040, which was introduced by the Loudoun County School Board for debate on June 22, 2021.

Despite a relatively boring title, the policy had the potential to do massive damage. It had been put forward by the very far-left ideologues whose names were on my petition for removal.

The policy, which has since become official in Loudoun County Public Schools, would require teachers to "allow gender-expansive or transgender students to use their chosen name and gender pronouns that reflect their gender identity without any substantiating evidence, regardless of the name and gender recorded in the student's permanent educational record."[1] It also stipulated that students should be allowed to use the bathrooms and locker rooms that "correspond to their gender identity."[2] A regulation, quietly issued after the passage of the policy, prevented parents from knowing if their child was claiming to be the opposite sex in school unless the child authorized the school to inform the parents. Think about that—a seven-year-old girl could change her name, her pronouns, and her identity at school and keep it secret from her parents, and the school would keep it a secret if that's what the seven-year-old wanted.

When this policy was being debated, we knew there was a miniscule percentage of kids in Loudoun County who were suffering from true gender dysphoria. They felt like they were born in the wrong bodies. Transitioning to another gender was probably the answer for them. Those kids deserved respect, and they deserved to be dealt with in unique ways on a case-by-case basis by the school.

Policy 8040, however, assumed that any kid who *said* they were feeling like a different gender—even if it was just today, even if they changed every 10 minutes—must be trans or gender expansive or whatever other label, no questions asked. That child, according to the bill, had the right to be addressed by a different name and gender by all school faculty simply because they demanded it.

While the bill was being debated, *The New York Times* (pretty much the Bible for white, well-off liberals in Loudoun County) published an explainer piece called "What Are Neopronouns?" In this article, the author explained that "a neopronoun can be a word created to serve as pronoun without expressing gender, like 'ze' and 'zir.' A neopronoun can also be a so-called 'noun-self pronoun,' in which a pre-existing word is drafted into use as a pronoun. Noun-self pronouns can refer to animals—so your pronouns can be 'bun/bunself' and 'kitten/kittenself.' Other refer to fantasy characters—'vamp/vampself,' 'prin/cess/princesself,' 'fae/faer/faeself'—or even just common slang, like 'innit/innits/innitself.'"[3]

So there was *that*, right in the pages of the newspaper that had published the Pentagon Papers, among other things. Clearly, the elite institutions of our country were being captured by this dangerous gender ideology. It was too late to stop the takeover at *The New York Times*, and it was definitely too late to stop it at most of our major universities. But we still had some time to make sure it didn't get into our public schools.

If we didn't, we all feared the consequences. By the time the policy was being debated, there were many stories about children who had claimed to be transgender at the age of five or younger and been encouraged in that delusion by their parents. There were stories about how those children were given hormones to stop puberty from taking place and then given surgery to permanently alter their sex organs. And in many cases, these children suffered horrible depression that occurred after that decision was made—children who regretted getting caught up in this trendy social movement for the rest of their lives and some who were forced to "detransition."

Many people learned these things from a book called *Irreversible Damage: The Trans Craze Seducing Our Daughters*, which was deemed so dangerous by the woke mob that Target was forced to pull it off the shelves. But the book told countless stories, all recorded by the author Abigail Shrier, of kids who should have at least taken a few years before making drastic decisions about their health that would affect the rest of their lives.

And many of them had made all these decisions *before* the trans issue became so popular. Shortly after its exposé on pronouns, *The New York Times* reported that "the number of young people who identify as transgender has nearly doubled in recent years, according to a new report that captures a stark generational shift and emerging societal embrace of a diversity of gender identities."[4] The number, according to the article, was only growing, especially among kids between the ages of five and 17.

I don't think any of the parents in our movement were suggesting we move off our strategy of focusing on the conduct of school board members, especially as it related to the enemies list. What we *were* suggesting was that everyone sit down, take a breath, and have a conversation before we rushed into accepting kids at their word about something as serious as "gender identity."

On a less serious note, I had been to high school. I knew what kind of trouble you could get into if you told kids that they had the power to change the names their teachers called them at will. If Policy 8040 existed when I was a kid and anyone could identity as anyone, you would have had a lot of "Joe Montanas," "Princess Leias," and "Optimus Primes."

Hell, when I was five years old I actually thought I could be Superman. I even tried to lift my dad's 1974 Mustang. In the process, I got a hernia and had to have surgery. When I got home, my grandparents gave me a get-well gift—the Millennium Falcon. My dad told me to stop being an idiot and that I wasn't Superman no matter how badly I wanted to be.

And don't even get me started on the gender identity piece of it. Were the teachers of Loudoun County really ready to keep track of which kids need to be addressed by "xim" and which ones needed to be called "cat" or "muffin?"

Given what I'd seen from this school system already, it didn't seem like it.

And if that sounds funny to you, consider that there is nothing in Policy 8040 that prevents any of it. Under the rules set forth in that document, when a kid tells you his or her name, *that* is his or her name, "regardless of the name and gender recorded in the student's permanent educational record." When a kid tells you his or her (or catself's or vampself's) gender, then *that* is his or her gender. Any teachers who even stopped for a moment to ask if the kid was serious could be subject to disciplinary action.

Not to mention that all this new social justice infrastructure would probably take away from reading, writing, math, and so on.

Which, allegedly, was what the kids were in school to learn.

Of course, any parents who spoke in opposition to this law were usually labeled bigots or transphobes (and usually racists, too, for good measure) by the school board and other parents. People were told that their fears about allowing boys of all ages into the same bathrooms and locker rooms as our daughters was not only wrong but hateful, too.

But the content of the policy was so outrageous that a few parents and teachers couldn't help but speak up against it.

One of them was an elementary school gym teacher named Tanner Cross who would soon become a hero.

THE CROSS INCIDENT

On May 26, 2021, Tanner Cross was one of many people who spoke during a school board meeting. Most were there to talk about critical race theory, the enemies list, or the school's masking policy.

But Tanner, as it turned out, had something else to talk about: Policy 8040. He had the facts on his side and a powerful way of speaking that made it hard to disagree with what he was saying. He also had empathy, which is always important when you're trying to get your point across in crowded rooms like the school board's meeting space.

When he got to the microphone, he was sure to say that he was "speaking out of love for those who suffer with gender dysphoria." Then he mentioned a special that had aired on *60 Minutes* about kids who had transitioned from one gender to another and grown to seriously regret it, all of whom were now in the process of "de-transitioning."

His short, powerful speech closed with these lines:

"I'm a teacher, but I serve God first, and I will not affirm that a biological boy can be a girl, and vice versa, because it's against my religion. It's lying to a child. It's abuse to a child. And it is sinning against our God."

Unfortunately, I didn't hear the speech in person. I was outside the school board building holding a press conference with Fight for Schools. I had been doing some more investigation into the report issued by the "Equity Collaborative" about the runaway slave incident in our district, and I had learned a few shocking things. Things that hadn't been made public before.

Essentially, the report detailed how the "Runaway Slave Game" at Madison's Trust Elementary in 2019 was an anti-racist exercise called the Underground Railroad Simulation. It was approved by the school and was an exercise that had been used for years by anti-racist educators and coaches.

When one person complained to the NAACP Loudoun, the head of that organization raised hell in the media. The teachers got thrown under the bus by LCPS, who then threw a boatload of money at the Equity Collaborative, which came in and wrote a garbage report which was then used to launch a Virginia AG investigation into LCPS, with the latter then willingly settling with the AG. A true sue-and-settle.

After four pasty white members of Chardonnay Antifa tried to derail our press conference by yelling and screaming how we were all racist, we delivered the report for the media. It got a little bit of coverage but was just too complicated to get much airtime.

In the aftermath of Tanner's speech, no one in Fight for Schools was talking about it. It was just another speech. Most people, including me, didn't know Tanner from Adam at that point. In fact, a lot of people involved with Fight for Schools were a little reticent about opposing Policy 8040. Heck, they'd already been called racists; they didn't really want Chardonnay Antifa now coming after them and calling them anti-gay, transphobes, and so on.

Two days after Tanner's speech, that all changed when I received a call from former Congressional candidate and my neighbor, Aliscia Andrews.

She broke some insane news about Tanner Cross. Apparently, Tanner had been placed on administrative leave after his speech to the school board. He had dared go against the woke orthodoxy, and he was being punished.

"We need to light the school board up," she said.

I received a few other similar calls and ended up putting in a call to Angela Cross, Tanner's wife. I asked her permission to go do my thing and go after LCPS for what it had done. She was very nice and very committed to her faith and said that they would appreciate the help.

In hindsight, and we have since laughed about it, I don't think she realized what me "doing my thing" was like!

"DOING MY THING"

When I got home, I sent out a press release that was hot with anger.

LOUDOUN COUNTY SCHOOLS PUTS TEACHER ON LEAVE FOR SPEAKING AT SCHOOL BOARD

Loudoun County, VA—Just two days after Fight for Schools presented research showing that Loudoun County Public Schools threw two teachers under the bus by misrepresenting the Underground Railroad Simulation at Madison's Trust Elementary in 2019, they have just rolled another teacher in order to please their activist base.

Elementary School gym Teacher Tanner Cross was placed on administrative leave, pending an investigation, for EXERCISING

HIS FIRST AMENDMENT RIGHTS during the last school board's open comment period.

Unfortunately, several activists spent the day emailing School Board Member Beth Barts to complain about Mr. Cross in an attempt to ruin him.

Please help Mr. Cross by emailing letters of support to the school board. But be better than the activists trying to destroy others.

Keep all emails polite and substantive, but firm in your support.

It was a solid press release: short, sweet, and to the devastating point. I was also able to link the Madison's Trust story, where other teachers had been thrown under the bus by Loudoun County Public Schools. In short, I was building a narrative.

Angela was very upset with the rhetoric and didn't understand why I would make the connection to Madison's Trust. She hadn't seen the press conference and naturally didn't know the shocking details that had not been reported. Tanner also called me and asked me to take down a tweet I had posted with his speech embedded that was pretty fiery.

I was a little peeved. I thought, here I am helping them and they're asking me to change my tone? But then I thought to myself, this guy's job is at stake. He's been thrust into a cauldron of national press coverage that existed because of what Fight for Schools has been doing, but his issue is very separate and different. He and his family are trying to navigate a situation that will likely involve litigation.

Maybe they are right; maybe the arrogant, albeit funny,

Chardonnay Antifa attacks have run their course. Maybe the critical race theory focus has run its course. Maybe this is bigger. I talked about it in the fall of 2020—the First Amendment. We had a private Facebook group attacking the First Amendment rights of parents while they themselves were violating the First Amendment. Now we have an attack on the First Amendment rights of a teacher. This is a woke school board that is trying to suppress the rights of parents, students, and teachers with whom the members disagree. This is dangerous.

So I calmed down, realized the need for flexibility and collaboration, and started working on some new messaging. We had been hammering away on the enemies list and critical race theory for two months and had been very effective. But we couldn't get stuck in the mud with the same message over and over again. What happened with Tanner was everything we had warned about and everything we were fighting against. It was time to raise the conversation in a way that still fit within our overall strategy—the plotting against parents for standing up for what they believed in had turned into action by Loudoun County Public Schools, and a teacher was paying the price. This was a school system that did not respect the Constitution, the rule of law, or opposing viewpoints, and they were more than fine with their activists' allies doing their dirty work for them.

I later came to appreciate that the Cross family had as much to do with what happened in Loudoun County as anyone else, if not more. They put their very livelihood on the line for a cause they believed in. Without Tanner's stand, the parents' movement in Loudoun may very well have fizzled out.

But because of his bravery, I ended up getting a call from Jeremy

Wright, a teacher who had become a core team member of Fight for Schools. He would go to school board meetings every two weeks and hammer away at them for the critical race theory teacher training. He was a congregant at a massive church in Loudoun County called Cornerstone Chapel. Thousands of people would go there during one of three services on Sundays. We had been trying to get in there to collect signatures but hadn't been successful.

It was understandable. The effort to remove six school board members was a divisive issue in the community. People would have different motivations for keeping their distance, even if they were supportive. Teachers who wanted to sign the removal petition but were afraid of repercussions. Potential donors who didn't want to have their names publicly disclosed because it might hamper business with the county.

But now, Pastor Gary Hamrick was ready for Fight for Schools to collect signatures at Cornerstone for two Sundays. The reason? He had a member of his congregation whose name was . . . Tanner Cross.

This was big time. We had been plodding along getting signatures after May 8, and it looked to me like this was going to take a long time to complete. The opposition was saying that we would never get the signatures needed, and to prove them wrong, we would need some big events to get the signatures we needed before the end of the summer.

We now had space to collect signatures at each service on the Sunday after Tanner was put on leave and space to do the same the following week.

This is where the Army of Moms shone. Stacy and Beth did a great job organizing the event, but it was also the new faces of the Army, many of whom I didn't know very well, who executed the plan to perfection. On that first Sunday, we picked up enough signatures to bring our total over 4,000 and have over 30 percent of the required signatures for four school board members: Barts, Serotkin, Corbo and King. I also got to meet Tanner and Angela Cross. I profusely apologized for going overboard, but they were forgiving and kind and would prove to be two people who always made sure to buck me up whenever the tide started turning or to congratulate me after our team had a big win. The next day, we sent out our first release showing those numbers.

A week later, we returned to Cornerstone, collected another few thousand signatures, and sent out another update to the media and our growing email list. Now we were at 60 percent with Barts, 54 percent with Serotkin, and 42 percent with Corbo. We'd gathered 7,149 total signatures in one month. We were cooking with gasoline, and the opposition was scared.

I had always assumed that we would file our first case against Beth Barts. She didn't have institutional support from the school board or the local Democrat party, and she had already been disciplined by her peers. In short, she was on her own and would be the easiest target from both a political and legal perspective.

Once we started showing that we were making progress on signatures, Barts started pushing back against Fight for Schools on social media. The one thing I will say about Barts—I respected her willingness to fight back, something I never saw from the other school board members. She never came after me personally, but she was snarky and she was brash.

Barts's willingness to fight back while the others cowered made me think: we had unified a divided board when we announced the recall campaign against six of them. Now we were having success getting signatures, and it looked like a real possibility that we could file cases in court by the end of the summer. Let's divide and conquer by focusing on Barts in our signature-gathering efforts, our Freedom of Information Act requests, and our statements to the media. Perhaps we could bait the other school board members into pressuring her to resign, thereby getting a win without even going to court.

Either way, it was yet another way to not get stuck in the mud, to change our angle of attack, to zig where we had zagged.

JAZZ HANDS

Before we could get to that plan, however, we had another school board meeting to attend on June 8.

This was the first meeting since Tanner Cross had been suspended, and it was the first time since Covid that members of the public would be allowed back in to sit in the meeting room as opposed to waiting outside in the hallway.

But LCPS would have a surprise in store for that day that came, not from the parents, but from the Loudoun County Circuit Court. The previous Friday, Tanner's lawyers from Alliance Defending Freedom argued in court for his reinstatement. There was a rally planned at Cornerstone Chapel to greet him following the hearing, and Alliance Defending Freedom's Communications Director and Loudoun parent Mike Friel asked me to come speak. I had just returned from the Heritage Resource Bank event in Austin, Texas, that morning and was ready to roll with a new kind of speech—one that was short on Chardonnay Antifa but long on parental rights and the First Amendment. I kept in mind my conversations with Tanner and Angela, and doing so truly helped me hone a message that not only would work for this event but would be the cornerstone of the message going forward.

The rally was fantastic, and Tanner and his lawyer Tyson Langhofer arrived at the very end to update on the status of the hearing, where the judge said that he would rule early next week. One thing was clear to me after this and two weeks collecting signatures at Cornerstone—the movement was growing.

That certainly manifested itself at the June 8 school board meeting. The support for Tanner was overwhelming, with hundreds of new parents and teachers showing up in force. As if an act of God, just before the meeting Judge James Plowman of the Loudoun County Circuit Court ordered LCPS to reinstate Tanner during the pendency of the lawsuit and said in his opinion that the actions of LCPS were "malicious and unnecessary." Of the many new faces at the school board meeting, most were on our side and standing up for Tanner's rights or against Policy 8040. Then there were those supporting 8040 who trained their fire mostly on those opposing it. In essence, if you didn't accept that schools should bend over backward to push gender ideology on kids, then you were a horrible person. There were several speakers supporting the policy that were not from Loudoun County at all. This would become an interesting point later.

Once again, I was able to tweet two speeches that went almost as viral as Shawntel's did after the school board meeting in early May. One was given by a teacher named Lilit Vanetsyan, who gave a devastating takedown of critical race theory from an educator perspective, and the other was given by Xi Van Fleet, a Chinese immigrant who had lived part of her life in Mao's China. As had become par for the course, I tweeted the speeches, emailed the tweets to my press and supporters list, and watched as they both made several appearances on highly rated Fox News shows and generated significant television, radio, and print/digital coverage as a result of their speeches.

Speech, tweet video, email tweet, rinse, and repeat.

Now one thing that became apparent to me at my first in-person meeting was that the chairwoman, Brenda Sheridan, was not going to tolerate any clapping. Instead, she demanded we use "jazz hands," where we shook our fingers above our heads in approval. Clearly Sheridan was missing the fact that she was sitting at the epicenter of a parents' revolution, and they were going to clap.

That didn't faze her in the least, and she shut down the meeting for applause right before I went up to speak—convenient! The meeting came back into session, several parents did a coordinated read from a "Parents Bill of Rights" that I had worked on with Elizabeth Perrin, and the meeting eventually was completed without further incident.

But I already had a plan for how to have some fun at the next meeting. I was going to go up there, cite a few cases to argue that applause is a First Amendment right, and then tell her that we weren't doing jazz hands anymore. The trick would be to see if they were tin-eared enough to shut down a meeting because of applause, thus walking right into another potential First Amendment question that could be used in the removal cases.

I never was able to execute that plan. Turns out, I didn't need to.

WHEN THEY MOBILIZE, GO GUERRILLA

KEY LESSON: When you're going up against the status quo, they will find a way to mobilize their political power and legacy media. That's inevitable. What's *not* inevitable is how you respond. When they finally confront you in the air, morph into a guerrilla operation that maneuvers on the ground.

FALLOUT

In the first pages of this book, I told you about what happened when I first saw the video of Scott Smith getting tackled by police.

I thought we were done. We had owned the national media narrative up until this point. Sure, we had collected a lot of signatures on the ground, but everything had been driven by Rule Number 5—turning our fight into must-see TV. We had dominated the air war, and it was driving maximal attention to our cause without so much as a hiccup or mistake to interfere. But someone getting arrested at a school board meeting? The left's aircraft carrier was now en route, and they had the kind of next-gen aircraft that almost took out Maverick and Rooster in *Top Gun: Maverick.*

Over the next few days, my fears were confirmed. It appeared that someone who seemingly agreed with me—who would have endorsed everything about our movement—had just crashed a school board meeting, made a scene, and gotten himself arrested. With the way the national media was portraying the event, it looked like we were going to be branded as insurrectionists, alt-right agitators. That wasn't true, but with now-overwhelming legacy media coverage singing from the same sheet of music, it looked like we might have a tough time building that broad coalition of Republicans, Independents, and Democrats to fight alongside us.

But if I had learned anything over the past 10 years in politics, the first news reports and chatter are never about the truth. They're about spin.

Consider what happened when a group of kids from Covington High School got into a "confrontation" with Native American protestors or when Kyle Rittenhouse was charged with murder for defending himself during the George Floyd riots.

For years, there has been a bias in media against anything that is perceived to be conservative. In the eyes of many people who work at major media institutions—many of whom live in places like Loudoun County, Virginia, and share the politics of far-left neighbors—the world is divided between good people and bad people. The good people are the ones who attend Black Lives Matter marches, and the bad people want to "ban books" and "not teach accurate history."

As always, the best course of action after seeing a news story that seems questionable is to reach out to those involved. You'd be surprised how many people skip this step. People are generally good, and when you ask them for help, they'll be happy to give it to you. At least that's what I've found during the two years that I've been running Fight for Schools.

What follows is the real story about what happened to Scott Smith, which I never would have found out without a crack team of investigators working with me.

When Scott Smith arrived at the Loudoun County School Board building on June 22, he was already very near the end of his rope.

About a month earlier, Smith had gotten a call from the front office at Stone Bridge High School, where his daughter was in ninth grade. That morning, the voice on the phone said, his daughter had been involved "in an incident." She had, in their words, been "beaten up" by another student. The voice on the phone refused to tell Smith who had done the beating or why it had occurred in the first place.

So he went to the school to demand answers, just like any parent would have.

When he got there, he wasn't getting the answers to his many questions. In Smith's case, the questions were *Who the hell assaulted my daughter?* and *What are you going to do about it?*, which would seem reasonable given the circumstances. But in Loudoun County, Virginia, in the year 2021, those questions wouldn't get easy answers.

Soon, Smith would learn that his daughter hadn't been "beaten up" at all. Rather, she had been sexually assaulted in a girls' restroom by a boy in a skirt who, according to later interviews with his mother, would alternate between dressing as a girl and as a boy.

122

By this point, the school board had begun its plans to pass Policy 8040, which was designed to allow all students to choose their gender and their bathrooms at will, for months. Whenever parents had come forward with concerns that the open-door bathroom policy could lead to the sexual assault of girls by biological males, who, as a matter of science, had an immense physical advantage over them, those parents were dismissed as bigots.

Coincidentally, the sexual assault happened just three days before Tanner Cross gave his speech against Policy 8040. Two weeks later, at the June 8 school board meeting chronicled in the last chapter, the fight over the school's transgender policies and the school board's willingness to silence dissenters like Tanner continued. Several parents blasted the board for sacrificing bathroom safety in the name of gender ideology, all to accommodate a small minority of students while ignoring the objections of a vast majority of parents. Unlike past meetings, which had been virtual because of the Covid-19 pandemic, this one had a full audience. Every time someone made a point against the woke ideology of the school board, the room filled with applause that was almost deafening.

While that June 8 meeting was happening, Scott Smith sat at home wondering what to do next. He found it incredible that members of the community were being silenced and mocked by the school board for expressing concerns about bathroom safety when his daughter had been sexually assaulted in a bathroom a little over a week before.

For a while, he wondered whether to go public with his story at all. Given the rancor that surrounded the issue, any announcement he made was sure to go viral. For Smith and his wife, Jessica, who owned a local business and depended on local support for their livelihood, becoming a flashpoint in the Loudoun County circus could destroy them.

But as it became clear that the school board was almost certainly going to pass Policy 8040, brushing aside the hundreds of parents who had deep concerns about it, Smith decided to show up to the next school board meeting to see what was going on with this now-infamous school board.

Smith was just one of several hundred people who showed up, including the 250 people who registered to speak. To make matters worse, not all these speakers were from Loudoun County. In the weeks leading up to the meeting, I learned via social media that the Loudoun Country Democrat Committee was encouraging far-left activists from all over the state to come to the meeting. Clearly, these people knew that the parents of Loudoun County were not going to back down and that they weren't going to win on the merits of their arguments. Bringing in supporters from outside was the only chance they had of selling the narrative that there was overwhelming support for Policy 8040.

By the time the date of the meeting arrived, the school board building looked like the site of a concert. The parking lot was full of people who supported "transgender rights," many of whom had come from outside Loudoun. They held signs with slogans about "protecting trans kids" and "trans rights are human rights." Mixed in with them were large groups of parents who lived in Loudoun County, nearly all of whom were there to show their opposition to the woke agenda of the school board. To my surprise, I learned that the parents outnumbered the transgender activists about three to one. The meeting was also packed with national and local media. I certainly didn't get them there, so it was clear that the other side of the debate was finally mobilizing their forces and getting ready to fight it out on the airwaves.

A few days earlier, I had decided not to attend the meeting.

Ever since I found out that the school board was busing in supporters, I had the feeling that our opposition was finally going to engage, and in a big way. This policy was the crown jewel of Chairwoman Sheridan and other Democrat state senators and delegates, and it only made sense for them to use this meeting and debate to start generating negative press directed toward the parents who were showing up to protest these kinds of policies being enacted by taxpayer-funded public schools. We had consistently been showing up to these school board meetings and dominating the attendance and the narrative. Our opposition knew this and was going to put all its effort into using this against us by flipping the script and showing that more people supported it than supported us.

This is when I started to mull over the idea of Fight for Schools skipping the meeting entirely and redirecting the effort to collecting signatures in Leesburg to pass the 100 percent threshold to remove Beth Barts. Some of my team thought it was a good idea— that we could be walking into a potentially explosive situation and that, if things went wrong, Fight for Schools would take the blame. Others thought we needed to go; otherwise it would look like we were giving up.

Ultimately, we decided to split our forces. Some would attend the meeting, but about 15 of us would organize a door-to-door blitz in Leesburg.

In hindsight, it was at that moment that we started shifting our operations away from the "must-see television" air war and began operating almost exclusively on the ground. School would be over that week, and after the June 22 meeting, there wouldn't be another one until August 10. If we could spend that time finishing the job on signatures, we would be in the catbird seat by Labor Day.

Of course, if we were going to shift tactics, I wanted to have a press conference to set the narrative. We gathered in front of the media on June 21 wearing some amazingly horrible T-shirts that I designed (the Army of Moms took that privilege away from me after that), and I updated the press and two dozen onlookers on how close we were to finishing the petitions for Barts and Ian Serotkin. I said we were beginning "Operation Finish the Job," and we were going to spend the next two months doing exactly that. I also explicitly warned our supporters to be careful at the next day's school board meeting: don't engage or get riled up, say your piece, and then leave.

Of course, while Fight for Schools wouldn't "officially" be attending the meeting, we did send a mobile billboard with "Recall Beth Barts" on it, which drove around the parking lot a few times to raucous applause from the throngs of supporters there. While I was out collecting signatures, everyone who filed into that building had to see it. It was a tactic that I had learned while working on political campaigns. Some on the left were mortally offended by such a basic campaign tactic, which was unsurprising. These people are all about playing the victim and doing so with so little self-awareness that they miss opportunities to fire back in an effective way.

But what was surprising was Beth Barts's response to the billboard. She "thanked" us for it, said that maybe she needed to get her own mobile billboard, and left one of her patented laughing emojis. For the first time since this all started, I found myself a little confused. This was THE woke warrior on the school board right? The kind of person who has zero sense of humor and takes everything so seriously? I would later run a poll in Leesburg to test how many people approved of Barts and how many supported the removal. The poll showed us that we had significant bipartisan support for what we were doing, but she must have received the polling call as it was being conducted and posted some of the questions with another snarky response about how she answered them.

Around this time, I started to realize that Barts wasn't looking to be a perpetual victim like the Ashleys of the world—she was looking to beat us. Did that make me lose any of my drive to remove Barts from the school board? Nope. But it did show me that this would be a fight, and unlike the other school board members or Chardonnay Antifa, she had at least an instinctive feeling on how to play my game.

But as I was with my friend Erin going door-to-door in Leesburg collecting signatures while watching the meeting on my phone, Scott and Jessica Smith, with their daughter also present, had to endure what must have been an incredibly painful array of speeches at the school board meeting. Transgender activists, who had all been allowed to sign up early, filled the first 20 minutes or so with empty words about "respect," "love," and "dignity." They said anyone who disagreed with them was intolerant. One of them said she could "see the hate dripping from the followers of Jesus" in the room. To these people, bathroom safety needed to take a back seat to kids being able to choose their gender, and anyone who had a differing opinion was an intolerant bigot who should be named, shamed, and silenced.

The first 20 speakers or so were overwhelmingly in favor of Policy 8040, likely tipped off by someone that the school board was moving the sign-up day from a Friday to a Thursday. But after about 17 people, the speakers started to go overwhelmingly against the school board. Then former state senator Dick Black got to the podium and utterly blasted the school board. Senator Black is in his 70s and was an accomplished politician and lawmaker in his day. But on this day, he had his finest moment. He utterly destroyed the school board for what they had been doing—from school closures to critical race theory to Policy 8040. And when he concluded, the room burst into applause. The board members, who had already warned them once about what would happen if they refused to remain quiet and obedient, voted unanimously to end public comment.

So the lady who attacked parents as hateful followers of Jesus was allowed to say whatever she wanted to antagonize the audience, but the former state senator was not allowed to passionately denounce the government officials who were charged with overseeing our children's education. Roger.

The parents, understandably, were outraged. The vast majority of people who had signed up to address the school board, as was their right, were not allowed to do so.

After a few minutes of shuffling around, which I learned about via my iPhone while I was out collecting signatures, the parents began singing "God Bless America" and "The Star-Spangled Banner" together. Some of the parents who attended the meeting sent me clips, which I later posted on Twitter for yet another viral Loudoun County moment.

A few minutes later, one of the parents set up a portable PA system and allowed people to continue speaking. A small crowd of outside activists and parents, Scott Smith and his wife among them, huddled around the small speaker to listen. While the speakers spoke their minds, the parents and activists spoke with one another, moving around the chairs that had been set up earlier as they joined each other's conversations. Eventually Smith's daughter got in line to speak in this spontaneous public comment session.

Judging by the reaction I was seeing online to my updates from afar, it was clear that our school board meetings had become the hottest reality show in America.

Unfortunately, the reality that happened next would be surrounded by a sea of lies until October.

THE MATCH

As the speakers continued their impromptu speeches, the Smiths' daughter got in line to speak about her experience. It was then that Jessica Smith noticed a woman she knew who asked Jessica "whose side she was on." Jessica said she was certainly opposed to what had been going on in the schools with critical race theory and other issues, to which the other woman responded that nothing of the sort was happening in Loudoun County Public Schools.

It turns out that this agitator had been part of the "Anti-Racist Parents of Loudoun County" Facebook group, since rebranded by us as "Chardonnay Antifa." She had come to the meeting dressed in a shirt with a rainbow heart on it and knew the Smiths. At some point, Scott turned around and asked his wife whom she was talking to. Jessica said that "she thought it was her friend," and then an argument began between Scott and the other woman. Scott began telling her the broad facts about what had happened to his daughter. When he was finished, according to Smith's account of the incident, later given to a reporter at *The Daily Wire*, she "looked [him] dead in the eyes and said, 'That's not what happened.'"[1]

In typical Chardonnay Antifa style, this woke agitator pointed to Scott's shirt, which had the name of his business on it—"Plumb Crazy"—and said that she would ruin his business.

Smith lost his cool and called her a "bitch," and then a police officer walked up behind Smith and placed a hand on his shoulder. When Smith didn't walk away, the officer gripped harder. Soon, before anyone knew what was going on, the officer, concerned about the situation, tackled Smith to the ground. In the struggle, Smith's pants fell down and his shirt flew up over his stomach, leaving him in an embarrassing position for the many people who had whipped out their phones to take pictures of him. All the while, Smith's wife shouted, likely knowing that many people were trying to get the incident on video.

"This is what happens," she yelled. "My daughter was raped at school and this is what happens."

I had gotten back home by the time I first saw the video, which was sent to me by a parent who had witnessed the whole thing. We had collected about 200 signatures that day, and instead of relaxing, I was prepping for an appearance on Laura Ingraham's show to discuss what happened at the meeting.

Damn, I thought. This kind of confrontation was exactly what I had been afraid of. It's the reason I decided to take my group out to pound the pavement instead of waiting around for something crazy to happen. I had been working with the media long enough to know that it would only take one viral incident at a school board meeting to undo all the work that Fight for Schools had been doing since April.

For the next few days, it appeared that this is exactly what would happen. Images of Scott Smith with his stomach hanging out and his hands cuffed behind his back began circulating. The next day, they were on the covers of newspapers and home pages of websites. Shortly afterward, video footage of the incident was playing on cable news networks and commentators were warning about the "dangerous parents" who were coming to school board meetings intent on committing violent acts and intimidating board members into submission.

This, of course, was a lie. In fact, exactly the opposite was happening. Soon the world would learn the truth about Scott Smith and about his daughter and the boy who sexually assaulted her, who was moved to another school while awaiting trial, where he then assaulted another girl. They would also learn about the depths of corruption that were going on in school boards all over the country and the lengths to which these far-left administrators were willing to go to see their partisan political objectives achieved, all at the expense of our nation's children.

But at the time, we didn't know any of that. All we knew was that we, the parents of Loudoun County, were getting a whole lot of attention, and very little of it was positive. To make matters worse, after Smith was arrested, Superintendent Scott Ziegler, who had now shed the "interim" label and was our superintendent for the next five years, declared an "unlawful assembly," which he later admitted in court was completely outside his authority. When a man named Jon Tigges peacefully stated that he would not leave, he was cited for trespassing. So now we had two arrests at the June 22 school board meeting, and Chardonnay Antifa, with help from the national media, successfully started building the false narrative that parents had just staged some kind of insurrection at a school board meeting.[2]

After everyone was kicked out, the school board reconvened and started debating Policy 8040. Some very critical things were discussed, but we were not in the room to see the debate, and even if we had, we would not understand the significance at that time. At one point during the business portion, Barts asked Superintendent Ziegler whether Loudoun County Public Schools had "assaults in our bathrooms, in our locker rooms regularly."

Ziegler answered, but he didn't answer the question Barts asked. He could have said that that assaults do not **regularly** happen in our restrooms, but instead he made a definitive statement: "To my knowledge we don't have any records of assaults occurring in our restrooms." As he said that, the camera caught a high-level staffer named Asia Jones squirm and put her finger to her nose.

The body language alone should have put up a red flag, but no one would even notice it, and what it meant, for months.

THE SMITHS SPEAK

Shortly after the incident occurred, Chair of the Loudoun County Republican Women's Club Patti Menders managed to get in touch with the Smith family, and we all met and talked via a long Zoom call. They relayed the entire story to me, and I was horrified.

But I was also intrigued about how this might impact Policy 8040.

During the call, it wasn't clear if the assailant was transgender, gender fluid, or just a dangerous boy without the capacity to understand "no." But the Smiths were adamant that the boy was wearing a skirt when he sexually assaulted their daughter and that he regularly would go into the girls' bathroom with no issue.

I also learned that the Loudoun County Sheriff's Office was investigating and waiting for the rape kit to come back, but the Smiths felt that an open bathroom policy was dangerous and that Policy 8040 must be stopped.

On that particular Friday that we were talking, they wanted to go public. I told them that I wasn't sure that it would be possible get any media to report on this without a formal criminal charge, and they understood. But they also expressed their concern that because any charge would be in juvenile court, it would be sealed, and the public would never be able to find out. We also discussed that if they went public, it would get wrapped in a political maelstrom and they would inevitably be demonized by the left as opportunistic parents who were using a terrible situation for political purposes.

We agreed that time was of the essence. Loudoun County Public Schools was planning to pass Policy 8040 at its August 11 school board meeting, so if they were to take any action to try and impact the consideration of the policy, it would have to happen before then. Scott Smith was scheduled to be tried on obstruction of justice and disorderly conduct in district court on July 20, 2021, so we decided to reconnect after that.

This call only further convinced me of the new angle we were going to take for the rest of the summer—patience, a lower profile in the media, an ear to the grindstone, and an all-out effort to get into court by the end of August. With our door-to-door push collecting signatures in Leesburg on the day of the June 22 meeting, we were over 100 percent with Barts; now we just needed to get another 500 signatures for cushion.

That is exactly what we would do.

DO NOT STOP AT THE WALL

KEY LESSON: A battle will have ebbs and flows, but at some point, you will find yourself hitting a wall. External and internal dynamics will make it challenging to get past that wall into the green fields on the other side. When you inevitably hit that wall, explode through it.

ARROWHEAD STADIUM

The 2018 AFC Championship Game was played in freezing weather at Arrowhead Stadium in Kansas City. The ascendant Chiefs, led by the seemingly unstoppable Patrick Mahomes, were heavy favorites against an aging New England Patriots team that, despite being in the last two Super Bowls, was on the last legs of a dynasty.

In the first half, the Patriots dominated on both sides of the ball, stifling Mahomes and building a 14-point lead. But in the third quarter, the Patriots hit the wall. Mahomes found his groove, and the Chiefs came back to take a 21-17 lead. It seemed like every time Mahomes touched the ball, the Chiefs would score. In fact, that's exactly what happened in the fourth quarter.

Meanwhile, the Patriots were sputtering. Outside of one field goal, the Patriots made mistake after mistake and could not regain momentum, and it looked like they had run out of gas against a superior team in the hostile environment of Arrowhead.

But the Patriots were the definition of a team. They weren't always the most talented, but they were mentally tough and had a sense of togetherness that they would always draw upon in the most dire moments to come out on top.

While the Chiefs were scoring on every drive in the fourth quarter, the Patriots didn't melt. They regained their swagger and matched the Chiefs score for score, ultimately getting into overtime where they took the ball first, marched down the field, and secured another trip to the Super Bowl with a touchdown run and a 37–31 win.

In the summer of 2021, Fight for Schools would eventually hit a wall—and we would fight through it.

INDEPENDENCE DAY

When I was a kid, the Fourth of July was a big holiday. We'd typically hit Bonnet Shores Beach Club in Narragansett, Rhode Island, and hang out by the ocean all day. After taking a break from swimming, a bunch of us would travel over to the rocks and collect a bucket of mussels and find a handful of quahog shells—anyone who watched *Family Guy* would know that quahogs are giant clams, and the shells would litter beaches in the Ocean State. My mom would steam the mussels and use the quahog shells to put together an amazing stuffing of bread crumbs and clams with a little cocktail sauce added for more spice. After dinner, we'd go back to the water, run around with sparklers, and watch an amazing display of fireworks, marking the Fourth of July as a unique summer holiday where families and friends celebrated the birth of the United States.

During the summer of 2021, there were many options for Independence Day celebrations, but in Loudoun County, the biggest one would be in Leesburg. The town would get together and celebrate what the United States of America stood for: freedom, inclusion, and the necessity of respecting people with all points of view.

In my first meeting with Sharon Virts, who would become my biggest donor and strategic advisor, she suggested that we build a float and ride through the parade with the Army of Moms and our children. After the year we'd all just endured, this was more important than ever. During those long battles over whether schools would ever reopen and what could be taught in our children's schools, it was easy to feel like everyone in the country was at each other's throats. It got to the point where I would wake up every day, check my phone, and wonder what kind of hateful message was going to pop up on my Twitter feed first. Now that I had become the face of a movement that was standing against the establishment, I knew it came with the territory. But that didn't mean it was fun.

Especially when I received my first piece of hate mail. It was a badly designed graphic of the Antifa fist holding a wine glass, and the text read: "The Only Reason We Need To Fight For Schools Is Because Of You! It's Worth The Price Of A Stamp And Ink To Tell You That You Are Tuckems Wannabe Trash And A Cancer To This Community And Loudoun County."

Meanwhile, Jessica Mendez received a mailing to her workplace, with pictures of her all over a letter and claims that she was a racist. This occurred after Fox New had interviewed several parents at Jessica's house and, while they were interviewing her on the front porch, Edna walked by and gave two middle fingers to the camera. When Fox News ran the footage for a story about hostile neighbors attacking people who were opposed to critical race theory, Jessica sat for an interview. It wasn't long after that the attempts to get her fired began.

Needless to say, we all needed a bit of a lift as the post–June 22 attacks began to mount.

The weekend leading up to the parade, I spent a lot of time with the Army of Moms designing a float that would represent our movement. Emily Emschwiller bought all the necessaries from the store, and Carrie Michon provided the trailer that we would use to build the float and did most of the design work. The day before the parade, I joined Kay Greenwell, Erin Smith, Erin Dunbar, and Jamie Fortier at Emily's house to build the float. We had the assistance of my two daughters and Emily's three daughters, who became fast friends and ended up, to my horror, playing on the trampoline for hours. (I ripped my ankle to shreds on a trampoline at my daughter's third birthday and vowed never to go near one again.) In the end, the float we came up with was fantastic, if I do say so myself. It had a giant red, white, and blue star in the middle with those same patriotic colors donning the sides of the trailer, completed with bales of hay for the children to sit on. Emily's husband Adam took all five girls on a test drive around the block several times to their delight, and we were ready to roll in the parade the next day.

But I wondered if the Fourth of July would be the same after all that had happened. In recent years, I had seen enthusiasm for the holiday—particularly among my white, far-left, *New York Times*–reading, CNN-watching neighbors—gradually decline. I recalled watching coverage of President Trump as he planned to give a speech in front of Mount Rushmore on July 4, 2020. The nation had just been through a pandemic, and I thought that everyone would be able to come together and appreciate the sight of a president—however one felt about him—standing in front of four of our nation's other great presidents and giving a speech.

But that didn't happen.

Shortly before President Trump was set to touch down in South Dakota, a correspondent from CNN went on the air and said he "will be at Mount Rushmore, where he'll be standing in front of a monument of two slave owners on land wrestled away from Native Americans."[1] Similarly, a reporter from NPR had noted that it was hard to celebrate given that questions about systemic racism were "hanging in the air like the aftertaste of tear gas."[2]

Yikes. Whatever else people say about sanctimonious leftists, they can be a *huge* bummer, especially around the holidays. I ended up writing an op-ed about that in *The Washington Times* in the summer of 2020 in which I pointed out the dangers of cancel culture from people drunk on wokeness:

> In present-day America, however, this suppression comes not from brutal dictators, but from the people who use social media and other platforms to crowdsource their performative activism to suppress other points of view, pressure businesses into compliance and to publicly humiliate their neighbors for expressing a different point of view.

I concluded the op-ed with the following, which I maintain is the right way to debate political issues in the United States of America:

Read. Write. Speak up. Consider all points of view, come to your own conclusions, and respect the rights of others to do the same. Do not let others bully you into abandoning your points of view. And always be a fierce defender of the freedom of thought and speech.

Little did I know in the summer of 2020 just how I was predicting the difference between the approaches of the two sides that would be fighting a local battle in Loudoun County with national attention.

Needless to say, I was somewhat skeptical about our group riding down Main Street in Leesburg, Virginia, after so many months spent stirring up division in service of our cause. I wondered whether people would throw rotten fruit at us or maybe hold up big signs the way they did when we showed up at school board meetings. Especially after the events of the last meeting, when the school board meeting descended into chaos, I had my doubts. With all those images floating around, I wondered, did people think we were the bad guys?

The answer was a resounding no.

When the morning of the Fourth of July arrived, at least a dozen of our core volunteers walked alongside our red, white, and blue float. The stars sparkled in the morning sunlight, and a few dozen kids—some of whom were ours, some of whom were friends—rode in the trailer, waving to their parents in the crowd. Some of them were as young as three, which gave me hope for the future. I hoped they were making the same kind of memories that I did as a child going to parades and watching fireworks from my backyard. All three Republican statewide nominees—Glenn Youngkin, Winsome Sears, and Jason Miyares—stopped by the float to talk to the kids and stand for pictures us proud parents were hellbent on taking.

As the float eventually started rolling down the street, we passed out candy, always greeted by loud cheers, and even had some candidates for local office walk in step with us for a few blocks. They had realized the power of our movement, and they wanted to be part of it.

We didn't collect many signatures that day, but we were humming along just fine on that front between our door-to-door operation and pop-up signature tables all around the county. The real win here was that we had an amazing time, and by the end, we had all bonded as parents. I felt a rush of energy and heroism in our cause that I hadn't felt since collecting signatures at Cornerstone Chapel.

For a moment, it seemed that everything was going to be just fine.

GOOD TIMES, BAD TIMES

But it wasn't all fun and games.

With Beth Barts as our target and no school board meetings until the middle of August, our job became very simple. We were going to pour all our energy into getting that cushion of an additional 500 signatures in the Leesburg District of Loudoun County.

We were already over the number we needed, but we wanted to make sure we had as many as we could possibly get. That way, we would have protection against any shenanigans from Barts's lawyer, Charlie King. Looking at Charlie, you would never mistake him for some kind of powerful, big-time lawyer straight out of central casting. He was more of a Columbo type. He was a Republican who had once run for chairman of the Loudoun County Board of Supervisors but had lost a winnable race because an independent candidate entered the race and split the vote, allowing the Democrat to win. Over the years, he had drifted from the local party, and his representation of Barts had been the final straw for many of his former political allies.

But Charlie had one thing going for him in this case—he had successfully beaten back an effort to remove former Board of Supervisors Member Eugene Delgaudio. I pored over the case file and knew that he was cagey and that underestimating him would be fatal to our efforts.

More than once, we had discussed the possibility that once the signatures were in, King would comb through them and claim that some were either fakes, doubles, unreadable, or collected from people who didn't really exist.

Which should be a lesson to anyone trying to take on the system: always go above and beyond. They'll try a million ways to discredit your efforts, so be prepared. Our goal was not to collect the 1,184 signatures we needed but rather to collect at least 1,684.

As a result of our very targeted mission, Fight for Schools morphed as I had planned into a fully functional ground operation. There weren't quite as many press opportunities with board meetings and school being over for the summer, and I didn't seek them out during this time. That meant I would have the opportunity to focus on the mission without the distractions of planning for school board meetings, reacting to the latest screwup from Superintendent Scott Ziegler and the school board, or coordinating different people to appear in the media to get our message out. I could also focus on fundraising and building our legal strategy for the upcoming court battle.

After the Fourth of July parade, we had a fundraiser in mid-July. In a gesture of defiance to the cancel culture mob, we decided to hold it at Parallel, the wine bar that had almost been shut down by the online wackos after selling a "Drunk Wives Matter" T-shirt. This, if you'll remember, is also where I first learned about the infamous Anti-Racist Parents of Loudoun County Facebook group.

The fundraiser went well. There were about 100 people in attendance, and they were all happy to drink a little wine and eat the amazing comfort food and signature drinks at Parallel while also getting to hear from our guest speaker and the man that would become so important to the fight in Loudoun County—future Attorney General Jason Miyares.

In the end, we raised about $15,000. For a local PAC, that was no small feat. Granted, most of it had come from our biggest donor, Sharon Virts—the same person who had the great idea about the Independence Day parade. When we'd first met in June, I had spent a lunch telling Sharon and her husband Scott about our goals, and she had responded with enthusiasm and a hefty donation. She was a lifelong Loudoun County resident, a self-made entrepreneur, and an author, and she was plugged in with just about every political figure in the county.

But no matter where the money was coming from, the event was a success, largely thanks to former Virginia GOP Chairman John Whitbeck. He had reached out to me in April to offer his help raising money, and we had immediately hit it off. He had me on a pretty rigid schedule making fundraising calls, which were typically designed for candidates for office. And like those candidates, I *hated* doing that but slogged through it to make sure this fundraiser was a success.

As we moved past the fundraiser, though, things started to get a little tense. Our amazing team of volunteers was filled with people who had different skill sets. There was our hard-core team who, on their own accord, set up pop-up signature-gathering events or put together a team to go door-to-door and collected thousands of signatures. There were the people who would be willing to go on television or radio and risk being a public face but were able to hold their own despite limited experience. There were others who knew the policies and had an encyclopedic knowledge of what the school board had been doing over the past several years and could help with talking points and outreach to others in the community to help build our coalition.

But to keep all these dedicated and talented people on the same page, we needed someone who could operate like a campaign manager or a chief operating officer. Unfortunately, I was not that. I had always led from the front—going door-to-door in the heat, hosting weekend drinking meetings with the team, letting them know that they were an indispensable part of the movement, handling all the more complicated political issues and needles that needed to be threaded, and taking the slings and arrows that came with being the most recognizable name in the battle.

By late July/early August, however, we started to hit a wall. With so few events to bring people together for a common cause, there was less communication, and that resulted in less camaraderie. For me, Fight for Schools was supposed to be something that I did in addition to working to support my family, but it was becoming a full-time job, and never having really had to manage more than four or five people, I found myself failing at the task of delegating and managing people. No one blamed me for it because I was focusing so much energy on strategy, fundraising, media, and keeping us out of trouble while in an environment that was fraught with risks.

To snap us back into game shape for the upcoming school year, we came up with an event that could bring us all back together and execute a fun tactic that I had cooked up.

On August 8, two days before the school board would reconvene to debate and vote on the transgender bathroom policy, we brought a film crew to the backyard of one of our key volunteers, Amy Jahr. After the June 22 meeting, the school board put in place new rules out of "fear for their safety." Those rules included only letting 10 people into the building at a time, with only the speaker being allowed in the boardroom for public comment. They also turned the camera away from speakers prior to that June 22 meeting, realizing that too many people were going viral for their speeches and making the school board look like what they were—incompetent.

Therefore, we decided to convene about 40 parents to record our own public comment session in Amy's backyard. We would then livestream it during the meeting itself as a way to show the school board that for every plan they had, we had one as well. A reporter from Fox News also showed up, and they were going to do a story on this new tactic on the day of the school board meeting as we were streaming our own public comment simultaneous to the "official" public comment.

The plan went well, and I paid a production company a few

thousand dollars to edit and make it as professional as possible. We had had great success raising money with over $250K raised by this time, so I was willing to spend a little to try to reengage the community and the media going into the August 10 school board meeting where the board would almost certainly pass Policy 8040.

SWEATING AND MAKING THEM SWEAT

On the day of the August 10 school board meeting, it was hotter than Hades outside and the school board would hear debate on Policy 8040 before voting on it the next day. Given the chaos that had ensued during the last school board meeting, only 10 people were allowed inside the building at a time. Thanks to these restrictions, there were a dozen media outlets camped outside, all holding boom mics and full cameras. Whenever a group of people went inside, we would look to our phones, watch their speeches, and support them as they came back out of the building.

No one was allowed to go inside to use the bathroom or cool off. We had gotten pretty used to the heat while we were out walking the streets collecting signatures, but even with the heat, it was a good time. We stood around and chatted, waiting for our names to be called so we could go in and speak.

While we were waiting, I spoke at a rally outside the school board that Patti Menders had put together. I think I fired up the crowd by updating them with the numbers of signatures we had collected, but that was nothing compared to Senator Dick Black, who stepped up to the microphone knowing he had complete control of the crowd.

It wasn't the first time.

During the last meeting, Senator Black had gotten up in front of the school board, which was still reeling from the Scott Smith tackling incident, and said what we all knew to be the case: that the Smiths' daughter had been sexually assaulted in a bathroom at a Loudoun County High School by a "gender-fluid" boy. When I heard him say it, my eyes went wide. I mean, I knew it was true, but I wasn't expecting anyone to bring this up at that time.

Well, now that the story had been told, I assumed that with the media there this would be a bombshell. But it never materialized into actual media coverage.

For my speech, I would handle things differently. I had decided after the last time I spoke on June 22 that I was done talking about critical race theory. I was done "shining the spotlight of accountability" to try to generate must-see TV. Our greatest asset with the school board was now the fact that we were in their heads. They mistakenly believed that this was some paid effort to swing an election while Chardonnay Antifa thought that I had been sent by the GOP to Loudoun County to test an election strategy. The fact that they thought I was running some kind of covert ops was flattering, the reality is that their own actions had created a massive pushback, and I was just the one leading it. From now on, we would use their fear, ignorance, and confusion against them.

Channeling that, I took the opportunity to update the school board on the number of signatures we had acquired—for all but Beth Barts. We were now over 100 percent of where we needed to be, but I wanted a sense of mystery. How close were we? Had we made a mistake and needed to start over? But I also gave a very clear message: call on Barts to resign. I knew we were getting close to being able to file our case against her, and I had a theory

I wanted to test. I had spent countless hours preparing the facts of the case against Barts, and I was amazed at how hard Brenda Sheridan, Ian Serotkin, and especially Atoosa Reaser went after Barts before the private Facebook group incident. These were Democrats who had no problem officially sanctioning Barts with a public reprimand, a censure, and harshly worded public denunciations when issuing those sanctions.

But the things that Barts had been sanctioned for didn't come close to the kind of explosive situation caused by the activities of "The Anti-Racist Parents of Loudoun County." Barts was really the only school board member involved in that particular activity, though Reaser and Sheridan remained in the group afterward with Reaser leaving in August only after we exposed that "The Anti-Racists Parents of Loudoun County" had conspired to cause a "disruption" at Leesburg Elementary while Barts, Reaser, and Sheridan were still in the group

So why did the school board never take action against Barts? As I learned, the group was started in early September 2020, and its early members included local Democrat leaders and all six school board members. Barts eventually left before returning one day before the fateful enemies list day. Maybe the other five had more complicity than I thought. Maybe they knew that they couldn't take a public stand against Barts because their hands weren't clean either.

Well, this would be their last chance. If they did the right thing, perhaps we would only file against Barts. If they did nothing, then I it would increase my growing suspicion that when Barts had said "silence is complicity" in her non-apology, that message had been at least partially directed to them.

Of course, nothing that we could say would stop the board from passing the transgender policy. The next day, they eventually voted 7–2 to pass it, ignoring massive parent outrage and creating even more determination in the community to remove the six board members who didn't seem to understand what their job was—to represent and respect the views of the whole community, not just a loud minority of radical activists.

But one school board member, Jeff Morse, made me realize that I was right—that there was more to this private Facebook group than Beth Barts. Morse, a moderate Republican, used his time to speak publicly against Policy 8040 but also to blast the members of the school board who were part of a group plotting against parents, did not denounce the group's activities, and did not apologize to the community.

It wasn't going to change anything, but for a careful and reserved school board member like Morse to come out so vehemently against six of his colleagues told me we were on the right path.

EXPLODING THROUGH THE WALL

After that meeting, I started making definitive plans to file our case against Barts. I had always said that we would file by mid-September, and several on our team had reiterated that on social media. I even met with two of the local reporters and said that they could expect a filing before mid-September. I didn't say who, how many, or specifically that it would be in mid-September, but we had successfully sold that as a target date. The goal was to keep the school board and Barts's attorney Charlie King off guard by filing in the last week of August. To quote Sun Tzu, "All warfare is based on deception."

With that goal clear, Jessica Mendez and I went to meet with our attorneys and give them the marching orders. I wanted to file on August 25. The attorneys seemed very excited about our strategy—filing a full complaint along with the petitions as well as a motion to intervene on behalf of Fight for Schools and a motion to disqualify the Soros-backed prosecutor Buta Biberaj.

This strategy was crucial to our success. Biberaj was a Democrat who was fully connected to members of the school board and their social justice crusade. She had also been part of the Anti-Racist Parents of Loudoun County group and had even joined a conversation there when members were calling for "racist Tik-Tok videos" of children whose parents that they wanted to expose publicly—that had another cancel culture attempt written all over it.

Further, in neighboring Fairfax County, parents had just watched a year of work go down the tubes when a Soros-backed Commonwealth Attorney had recused and handed it over to another Soros-backed Commonwealth Attorney, who then voluntarily dismissed their removal petition even after the judge had said it could go forward.

We would have to avoid that scenario at all costs, and our attorneys seemed to understand.

I decided to keep my plans under wraps until the right moment. Luckily, I didn't have to wait long; the pleadings were ready for review by Monday, August 23.

Everything looked great—we had laid out a complete indictment of Barts in the complaint, and if we couldn't win this case, then the removal statute truly was toothless. I did have one question, though. Usually, when filing a complaint, a lawyer will sign the document and then be attorney of record. This then means that the lawyer will get any pleadings from the other side and could then communicate receipt back to the client. On this pleading, however, it only had a spot for a citizen to sign on behalf of the petitioners. I questioned that, and the next day they responded that they believed that was the best approach since this was such a strange type of action without much precedent. They were right about that—our approach was unique, the statute was vague, and there was no real precedent for even filing a complaint along with a petition.

Since I had already started to prime the pump with our team, the media, and our supporters, all while keeping our plans about Barts and the school board under wraps, I decided to roll with what they had given me.

Jessica and I went to the Loudoun County Courthouse and filed the paperwork before 2:00 p.m., took a selfie in front of the court-house, and proceeded across the street to the government building where we would be having a press conference announcing the fil-ing. On the way there, we walked by Barts's attorney Charlie King, who gave us a strange look of recognition. Did he know? Had he been tipped off? I don't know for sure, but the look he gave us was not one of expectation but surprise. It may have been coincidence that the lawyer who would be representing Barts walked by us at that moment, but he also may have had other business at court.

In any event, we proceeded to give the press conference, with around 25 supporters flanking me at the podium. Eventually, King showed up at the presser and watched as I read through the com-plaint much like a prosecutor announcing an indictment. After-ward, he came up and shook my hand. I honestly couldn't help but like the guy. He, like his client, had continually tweaked me in the press and on social media, but I respected that neither seemed to take it all that personally and that this was political battle where two sides were putting it all on the line to win.

That said, I still didn't take him all that seriously. We had as good a case for removing a school board member as the state had ever seen, and this was all going to play out during the most-watched political election in the country.

A week later, though, I would have to take him seriously. I was on my way to a senior living facility to talk to a crowd about what we were doing. While driving, I received a call that Leslee King, one of the school board members we were collecting signatures for, had passed away. She was in her late 70s and had recently under-gone heart surgery, and we had heard her health was failing. We hadn't made a final decision on what to do, but we had quietly stopped collecting signatures in her district.

What this also meant was that the school board would be select-ing a replacement for Leslee King, certainly before the election in November. With six Democrats and two Republicans, we didn't expect to get a reasonable replacement, but that was a strategy that would have to wait.

After I concluded my talk at the senior center, I received a call from a key volunteer named Mike. I had asked Mike to sign the pleadings because the lawyers had advised me that it would be bet-ter to have a citizen signer than a lawyer. Charlie King immediately seized on that and filed a motion for sanctions against Mike for signing a pleading as a nonlawyer along with a motion to dismiss based on the invalid filing.

Ordinarily I would have dismissed this as nothing more than desperation, but the fact was that I had had the same concerns about having a nonlawyer sign the pleadings. Now my concern had manifested itself in the case itself, threatening to undermine all our work and make our whole operation look unprepared and unsophisticated.

When I got home, the first thing I did was put out a statement about Leslee King, expressing sympathy for her family and friends. We may have disagreed with her policies or the fact that she had been in that Facebook group, but politics should never get in the way of humanity.

Afterward, I called our attorneys, and we discussed the complications involved with Charlie King's counterattack. They could not represent Mike because that could be a conflict so I immediately called David Warrington from Hameet Dhillon's firm, The Dhillon Law Group. He confirmed that Charlie King's argument was a viable one. We had been on offense all spring and summer, and now we found ourselves fully on defense.

I spoke to some other attorney friends, and they all confirmed what Dave had told me. I called Dave back and told him that I wanted him to take over, represent both Mike and Fight for Schools, and get us off the defensive and back on the offensive. He accepted and immediately got to work.

Meanwhile, I received an inquiry from the two Loudoun newspapers. Both were asking about the latest filing from Barts. It was well played by Charlie King—he even gave them a quote that "Fight for Schools and Ian Prior weren't ready for prime time." I carefully gave a comment back about this being nothing more than a distraction, but I was very concerned.

Those stories weren't terrible, but I did get some calls from donors and other supporters in which I had to explain the situation.

In the long run, I knew that this was not a huge deal from a legal perspective and that we would be fine, but King had used his experience in removal litigation to his advantage and was able to create a narrative that this was some massive screwup. It certainly had the effect of generating significant concern among our volunteers, board of directors, and donors, who were now losing a little bit of confidence in the plan.

To make matters worse, that week Jessica received a second letter at her workplace encouraging her employer to fire her for being a "racist" who hung out with "insurrectionists." The personal attacks were taking their toll, and now we had bad press making Fight for Schools look like it had dropped the ball with a big mistake in its first filing.

Something was going to have to be done to ensure that everyone was on the same page heading into the final stretch of September, October, and November. We were going to be in court in the Barts case, we had to complete all signatures by the end of election day, and we had to keep the momentum going so that Glenn Youngkin would have a chance to beat Terry McAuliffe.

This organization had been so successful. We had filed one case and were making progress to have the rest of the petitions done before Election Day. I wasn't going to let a few momentum shifts, miscommunications, and fear of failure destroy all of that. It was time for a come-to-Jesus meeting, which I set for a Sunday at my house.

To help fix things, I enlisted Paul Chen. He was on the board but was really focused on his role as a district chair for the local Republican party. Because of that, he wasn't really tuned into the day-to-day dynamics that had existed as the organization evolved from those early days. I asked him if he could be the moderator, and he said he would.

I was certainly not looking forward to the meeting. I realized that the problems were typical of these kinds of political operations in the dog days of summer. I faced the same dynamics when I was managing Brendan Doherty's campaign for Congress in Rhode Island back in 2012. There is a burst of energy when things begin, but as it gets into July and August, a sense of anxiousness sets in, which leads to conflicts, loss of confidence in the way things are progressing, and a feeling that the odds are insurmountable. But with September on the horizon, school board meetings starting up again, a court case, and an election, everything was going to start moving so fast the problems would resolve themselves—*if* we could reset for that final push.

But we got everything prepared, and most of the volunteer team and the board attended. It started off very vanilla, with Paul setting the parameters. At some point, the conversation drifted into how we could help get Youngkin elected, but Amy Jahr passionately stated that was not why she was in this, collecting signatures every day in the heat. She was in this to make changes to Loudoun County Public Schools, and she was right. But getting Youngkin elected would also help that happen.

Eventually the meeting started to get heated. Everyone there had been working their asses off since at least March, with some at it since the previous June. There was some finger-pointing, second-guessing, and a fear that everything we had done could be for nothing. With so many different personalities, this is normal. Disagreements on how to do things had been bubbling up since late June, but I had largely ignored them in the naive hope that the problems would solve themselves.

While I was listening to the discussion, I was thinking about that 2018 AFC Championship game. We had all the momentum and built up a big lead. But we had given our opponents an opening. While not our doing, the June 22 school board meeting had given them the ability to brand us as horrible, right-wing insurrectionists. Meanwhile, a mistake in filing the Barts case had given them the narrative that we were amateurs. It was taking a toll, and it felt like we had fallen behind. But we were headed into the fourth quarter, we were still in the game, and it was time to explode through the wall.

With no warning, I just yelled: "Enough! We all need to cut this shit out right now. We are on the precipice of either a massive failure or a historic success. We have accomplished more than anyone thought possible, and while everyone has contributed so much, if we fail, I'm the one that is going to have the most egg on his face and take the public blame for the loss. Well, I don't plan on that happening. I am sorry if I have failed in any way up to this point, but right now we need to focus forward, saddle up, finish the job, and if we succeed, we might just change the course of the election."

I kept going for what seemed like five minutes but was probably far less. I had never really showed any emotion throughout this fight. Sure, in school board speeches I had brought the occasional fire, but in dealing with people face-to-face, mostly I was always calm, friendly, and looking to de-escalate any and all conflicts. Looking around, the room was dead silent. Maybe they felt that I was as stressed as them, as scared of failing as them. Something that I never wanted to show—vulnerability—may have been the one leadership moment that could get everyone motivated to break through the wall and finish the game.

Whatever cloud had been hovering over our team since that June 22 meeting was gone. You could feel that everyone had a new sense of purpose, a new energy, a new vigor to spend the next two months doing whatever it took to win in court, finish gathering signatures, and maybe even inspire the whole Commonwealth of Virginia to elect a governor who would start putting parents before special interests.

Even I had a new sense of my purpose in this fight. I could see the light at the end of the tunnel. There was a date certain to complete the mission: November 2. Everything that happened between now and then would require us to be mentally tough and handle any situation with the perfect strategic action while also using the skill set of every person who had put so much into this effort.

As it turns out, that's exactly what we were about to do.

RULE NO. 9

YOU'VE GOTTA BELIEVE

KEY LESSON: All the creative ideas, strategies, and tactics mean nothing unless you believe in your cause and believe that you can win. Be flexible and open to ideas, but never take your eyes off the North Star and never forget why you joined the fight in the first place. Only then can you find yourself in the endgame you were destined to win.

THE NORTH STAR

From July 2020 to March 2021, I came to know certain things:

I knew that a dangerous strain of cancel culture was taking root in communities and neighborhoods.

I knew that our public schools had been captured by special interests and were determined to implement wokeness, even if the cost was high-quality education.

I knew that far-left activists, like the members of Chardonnay Antifa, were dangerous to those they viewed as opponents and were a liability to those they saw as allies.

I knew that the Virginia statewide election in 2021 would attract significant national attention as it was the first election since Joe Biden was elected and was the only predicted competitive election in the country.

That knowledge led me to certain beliefs:

I believed that exposing the activities of far-left activists in the "Anti-Racist Parents of Loudoun County" would be an important first step to push back against the raging cancel culture commandos who used victimhood to try to destroy lives.

I believed that the six school board members who were part of that group had destroyed trust with their constituents because of their membership in that group and failure to denounce it—trust that was already on thin ice following school closures.

I believed that, through a campaign to collect over 17,000 signatures to remove those six school board members from office, we had an opportunity to ride the wave of political coverage of the elections to bring attention to our cause and the cause of others who had woken up to the politicization of our public schools.

I believed that our best case would be against Beth Barts and that we would be successful.

Finally, I believed that the problems with Loudoun County Public Schools went far beyond one school board member and that when faced with pressure from the community, the school board, the administration, and their political

159

allies would make significant mistakes that would only further confirm that the Educational Industrial Complex was broken.

But it wasn't enough for me to believe those things; I needed others not only to believe them as well but also to believe in me. To follow my lead, to trust my untested plan, and to go the extra mile to execute it.

It wasn't always sunshine and rainbows, but as the summer of 2021 turned into the fall, all those beliefs turned into reality.

THE GAFFE

As the weather got colder through the fall of 2021, the race for governor started to heat up. While I hadn't seen Glenn Youngkin since he spoke at a fundraiser we had in September, he was gaining in popularity among people I spoke with. They believed he was our best chance of ensuring freedom from the tyranny of the Educational Industrial Complex in Virginia.

But the polls did not agree with me. In September, Youngkin was consistently down anywhere from four to seven points in the polls, leading to fears on my part that our movement would be demoralized after the election. I wondered what would happen if Terry McAuliffe, his opponent, ended up in the governor's mansion. For months, the McAuliffe campaign had made it clear that they thought our movement was nothing but a conspiracy theory.

Meanwhile, Youngkin was beginning to strongly embrace the parents movement. In the beginning, I didn't get the sense that the

Loudoun County fight was going to be a key piece of his campaign. I don't blame him. Back then, I'm sure we seemed like a disorganized bunch of angry parents who wanted to show up and give speeches at school board meetings. There didn't seem to be much benefit in focusing on one county in Virginia because of a few viral moments at those meetings.

But now, with Youngkin fully backing parents, every event that he did had an audience of people who were fully engaged in the parents' rights movement and saw what was happening in Loudoun County as an inspiration. They cheered louder, raised their hands higher, and showed up in far greater numbers than the other side. (No matter what else is wrong with the woke moralists on the other side, they're not nearly as fun as the parents' rights folks.) Slowly, it seemed that the battle lines were being drawn, and we were right in the middle. The race for the governor's mansion in Virginia was going to center on the issue of parental rights, an issue that was becoming synonymous with two words: Loudoun County.

Within the movement, things were moving smoothly. Once we had exploded through the wall and out of the dog days of summer, we started cooking with gasoline. Our first court hearing in mid-September was virtual and lasted about five minutes because the judge had to recuse himself. The rescheduled hearing went forward two days later with a new judge, Jeanette Irby. Again, I reached out to get intel on Judge Irby, and it was mostly positive. She was a no-nonsense judge who would focus on substance, not technicalities or theatrics.

That readout couldn't have been more correct. From the outset, she seemed skeptical of Charlie King's approach, and this skepticism turned into visible impatience. The hearing turned out to be just a scheduling call, but from the judge's tone, it looked like King's gambit to get the whole thing tossed because of the filing mistake would fail.

The judge scheduled the motions for October 6, and we would have our day in court.

Meanwhile, early voting had begun in mid-September, and our volunteers were out at the location every day, collecting hundreds of signatures a day. By the end of September, we had gathered enough signatures to pass the threshold for two more school board members: Ian Serotkin and Denise Corbo. All that remained were finishing off the chairwoman, Brenda Sheridan, and the vice chairwoman, Atoosa Reaser. Those petitions had been harder because they represented eastern Loudoun, which was not only far more Democrat-leaning but also an area where very few of our volunteers lived or could get to easily. But an early voting location would open in Sterling in mid-October, and we were confident that we could finish off those last two petitions by staffing those locations and some voting locations on Election Day.

Finally, school board season was upon us again. The September 28 meeting would bring a surprise guest: *The Daily Wire*'s Matt Walsh. Patti Menders had been able to get him to come to town for a rally and to speak at the meeting. Walsh had given a viral speech at school board meeting in Tennessee, and Patti had had the great idea to bring him to Loudoun and generate more news.

Once the school board got wind of this, they made a rule change—only Loudoun residents or business owners could speak. I did a quick bit of research and determined that this action, while legal on its face, could be a First Amendment violation if the goal was aimed at stopping Matt Walsh from sharing a viewpoint that Loudoun residents wanted to hear. But it became a moot point for the time being because Walsh hilariously ended up leasing a room at Patti Menders's house for $1 and used that fact to further mock the ridiculousness of the Loudoun County School Board during his media tour before and after his speech.

As the school board meeting began that afternoon, there were around 500 people packed into the parking lot to watch a list of speakers that included Walsh. I spoke first and then rushed off to coach my six-year-old daughter's soccer practice before returning to the event to deliver public comment. Walsh gave a blistering speech against the school board for the danger they were creating to children by passing the transgender bathroom policy, and his appearance in Loudoun and his speech would later be featured in his documentary *What Is a Woman?*

But the biggest news that night wasn't from the Loudoun County rally or school board meeting. It wasn't revealed to us until we were having drinks at a restaurant next to the school administration building. While people were socializing at the bar, I was checking my Twitter feed when I saw a clip of the Democratic candidate for governor, Terry McAuliffe, saying at a debate that "parents shouldn't be telling schools what to teach."

WOW!

With everything that had been happening in Loudoun County, McAuliffe had just made the worst possible statement. He had just given the Youngkin campaign immediate television ad fodder and everyone in Virginia would see it, with only the most dogmatic leftists agreeing with it. Much like what had happened with Tanner Cross, this would bring even more people into the parents' movement, and this statement would be hung around his neck until Election Day.

Over the next few days, things would get even worse for McAuliffe and the Loudoun County School Board.

DOMESTIC TERROR

On October 4, Attorney General Merrick Garland issued a memo instructing the FBI and United States Attorneys to investigate a supposed "disturbing spike in harassment, intimidation, and threats of violence against school administrators, board members, teachers, and staff who participate in the vital work of running our nation's public schools."[1]

Mere days before the Garland memo, the National Association of School Boards had sent a memo to the Biden administration asking that it deploy federal law enforcement and counterterrorism agencies to investigate parents at school board meetings, including by using the domestic terrorism provisions of the Patriot Act.[2] They cited the threats to school board members and parents who engaged in harassment and intimidation. They cited several "examples" in their request, including a link to Scott Smith's arrest at the June 22 school board meeting. (They did not mention, of course, that no one had ever been physically harmed at a school board meeting or that Mr. Smith's daughter had been sexually assaulted in a bathroom.) But with the language they used, you would have thought that parents were breaking down the doors of school board buildings with flamethrowers under their arms and then tying up school board members and physically attacking them.

That's certainly how Merrick Garland seemed to interpret it.

Garland would further warn in his memo that "while spirited debate about policy matters is protected under our Constitution, that protection does not extend to threats of violence or efforts to intimidate individuals based on their views."

Now, I should pop in here and say that as the representative for one of the most prominent parents' rights group in the country—and the kind of person at whom this letter was obviously aimed—I had seen absolutely no threats of violence at school board meetings. As you've seen through the pages of this book, my parents' rights group came together to petition our local government for a redress of grievances, as was our right under the Constitution, and we just so happened to have a great time doing it. Yes, we would call out elected officials for what they did and said in their capacity as elected officials. We were able to shine a national spotlight on the Loudoun County School Board. We took advantage of every mistake the board members and superintendent made and highlighted that in the media. Metaphorically, we hit hard and often, but always within the rule of law and the unwritten rules of politics.

In response, we'd been labeled enemies by our peers, called every name in the woke playbook, and called out on social media daily for our supposed crimes against the regime. The intimidation was only coming from one direction. And now, with Merrick Garland's memo, that intimidation was coming right from the White House.

It's not like Garland's memo was a soft finger-wagging to parents, either. It was a threat.

"The Department takes these incidents seriously," he wrote, "and is committed to using its authority and resources to discourage these threats, identify them when they occur, and prosecute them when appropriate. In the coming days, the Department will announce a series of measure designed to address the rise in criminal conduct directed toward school personnel."

In the weeks to come, a few lawmakers would comb through the evidence for this "violence" that the National Association of School Boards had presented in its memo. No one who'd been paying attention was surprised that of the 15 incidents they'd cited, not a single one had involved the kind of activity that merited a full-throated response from federal law enforcement.

But the NSBA didn't give up. Shortly after the memo, the organization's interim CEO said the letter was "a strong message to individuals with violent intent who are focused on causing chaos, disrupting our public schools, and driving wedges between school boards and the parents, students, and communities they serve. The individuals who are intent on causing chaos and disrupting our schools—many of whom are not even connected to local schools—are drowning out the voices of parents who must be heard when it comes to decisions about their children's education, health, and safety."

I wondered, as I had many times during the past year, on what planet this guy was living. During even the most heated school board meetings, most of the people who'd come from outside the community were the ones trying to support the school board and pass policies that were deeply unpopular with parents. To the extent a few people—other than Matt Walsh—came from "the outside" to speak at a school board meeting, they had been from neighboring Fairfax and Prince William Counties and were simply linking arms to show unity with their neighbors in Loudoun.

During this ordeal, I would often check the national temperature on the issue of parents' rights. Not that I needed to look very hard. It seemed that every day, someone was making a statement about it. There were debates in Congress, op-eds in major newspapers, and 10,000 fights on Twitter a day. Every once in a while, someone would mention me, Fight for Schools, or "Loudoun County Parents," by name, and I would take a moment to be amazed at how far our small, ragtag group had come since I came up with the idea in my basement.

Whether it was Tucker Carlson, Laura Ingraham, Dan Bongino, or even former President Trump, the eyes of the nation were on what was happening in Virginia. That's right—in an interview with Fox News, President Trump said this when discussing how parents would impact the 2021 Virginia election: "I've been watching the school board hearings more closely than I ever have, to be honest, and it's so interesting. The parents are incensed. They're not terrorists, they're just people that are so upset. They're angry, they're hurt, they're crying because their children are being taught things that, in our opinion and in my opinion, and a vast majority of the people in this country's opinion, they don't want their children to hear about this stuff.... They want to go back to reading, writing, and arithmetic."

This outraged parents, who were now watching what was clearly a coordinated political campaign to shift the narrative and label as domestic terrorists those frustrated parents angry about government-sanctioned transgender activism in schools, open bathrooms, critical race theory, and vaccine and mask mandates.

For me, this opened the floodgates for media appearances. As I was a former deputy director of Public Affairs at DOJ and now the leader of the biggest parents' movement in the country, my phone was blowing up with offers to go on television, radio, and podcasts and give interviews to various media publications covering this major story. Since every TV or radio hit led to money for Fight for Schools to pay for our removal efforts, I was more than happy to do it.

During these appearances, I tried to be as funny and affable as possible. But I always tried to give credit to the organization and the parents doing the hard work. In early October, I went back on *Tucker Carlson Tonight* to discuss the Garland memo and asked if a "mean snarky tweet" was going to get me or others investigated by the Justice Department and that when I worked there "we investigated MS-13 and now they want to investigate moms of 13-year-olds." It wasn't another Chardonnay Antifa moment, but I got the point across—the Justice Department was attacking the First Amendment rights of parents, and it was going to backfire.

VINDICATION

But while this was all happening, we were gearing up for our October 6 hearing in the Barts case. Around 20 Fight for Schools supporters and volunteers showed up, including my wife! She usually kept a low profile, but she knew that this was going to be a big day in the grand scheme of everything we had worked to achieve. We were nervous but hopeful. If we succeeded in disqualifying

Commonwealth Attorney Buta Biberaj as the "prosecutor," we would stand a real chance of winning the first removal trial of a school board member in Virginia.

Right from the beginning of the hearing, I was confident. Our supporters flooded the courtroom, while only one woman—wearing a BLM mask—was there to support Barts. Where was the Chardonnay Antifa crew who had put her in this position in the first place? Absent. Where was the local NAACP whose "anti-racism" efforts certainly aligned with Barts? Absent. Where were Barts's supporters from the Democrat party? Absent. They had thrown her to the wolves, letting us do the work to remove her while they hid in the shadows, hoping that their own complicity in these battles would be washed away with Barts.

Meanwhile, Barts's lawyer Charlie King was trying to argue that our petitions were invalid because our affidavit section was "missing a colon." Biberaj, who as the Commonwealth Attorney was supposed to be prosecuting the case against Barts, was taking King's side in this argument. The judge was clearly not buying it and denied the motion to dismiss.

After taking the stand to establish a foundation for why we needed to intervene, I was cross-examined by both King and Biberaj. King was generally fine, but Biberaj just reeked of seething anger. She was going overboard to keep us from intervening so that she could kill this case. I handled it generally well, and shockingly, we won that motion as well. We were now in the case.

That allowed us to argue the motion to disqualify Biberaj. Our attorneys were able to introduce evidence of her on social media tweeting out an article that accused us of being liars and rabble-rousers, but beyond that we couldn't get our other evidence admitted.

Our lawyer Dave Warrington argued that Biberaj's own conduct during the hearing on the motion to quash was evidence that she was biased against our case, and the judge agreed, disqualifying the Soros-backed prosecutor and telling us that she would appoint an independent prosecutor to handle the case.

We were in disbelief. We had won every single motion. The odds greatly shifted in our favor, and discovery would be a nightmare for Barts, the rest of the school board, and the woke babies of Chardonnay Antifa who thought they were invincible.

Outside, the team coincidentally ran into Scott Smith, who was there for a hearing in the case involving the sexual assault of his daughter. He was ecstatic to see Biberaj walk out of court a loser, as it had been Biberaj who personally prosecuted Smith for disorderly conduct at the school board hearing where he was arrested. After doing a few interviews with local and regional media, I joined the Fight for Schools team at a local bar for a quick drink before heading to the Fox News studio to talk about where things stood in Loudoun County.

This was a massive win. I could feel the energy from the team of hardworking moms who had spent hundreds of hours collecting signatures, speaking at school board meetings, walking in parades, attending rallies, and bonding over a common mission. It had also validated the trust that they had put in me as their leader, which would come in handy two weeks later when I needed them to move mountains once more.

Supporters all over the state called to congratulate us, especially from neighboring Fairfax, where they had not been as successful in their efforts. To show solidarity with the Fairfax parents, as they had done for us by showing up at the press conference where we announced we had filed on Barts, I agreed to attend a rally they were holding ahead of their school board meeting the next day.

TRUTH AND LIES

As I was driving to the Fairfax rally the next day, I received an emailed press release that would set in motion a chain of events that would put Loudoun County under the spotlight of accountability like it had never experienced, even over the past two years.

The email was a press release from the Loudoun County Sheriff's Office stating that it was investigating a sexual assault at Broad Run High School. It seemed strange that this would be sent out via press release, but I didn't give it much thought until I received a call from a parent asking me if I saw the release. Apparently, several people had been able to confirm that the boy who had committed the sexual assault at Broad Run was the same boy who had sexually assaulted the Smiths' daughter at Stone Bridge. He had been moved to a different school after he had been arrested and was awaiting trial while being allowed to attend school while wearing an ankle monitor.

This was a massive dereliction of duty by Loudoun County Public Schools, in more ways than one. Superintendent Ziegler had completely misled the public at the June 22 school board meeting about there being no sexual assaults in bathrooms.[3] No one on the school board had corrected the record. And the offender had been quietly moved to a different school where he had committed a second assault.

Why? Because the school board members had known that if they corrected Ziegler, the concerns about boys being allowed in

171

girls' bathrooms would be validated and would make it almost impossible to pass the policy. No one was saying that he had to give details of the Stone Bridge sexual assault. A simple "Yes, we have had sexual assaults in our bathrooms, but because of privacy laws we cannot share those details" would have done the trick for Ziegler.

But he didn't do that.

And if it had been an accidental statement, then a reasonable superintendent would have released a statement the next day saying: "I misspoke at the meeting. There have been sexual assaults in our bathrooms, but because of privacy laws we cannot share those details." But he didn't do that, nor did the school board, because regardless of whether the assailant was transgender, pansexual, polyamorous, or just a boy, the issue of bathroom safety was *the* theme of the opposition to the proposed bathroom policy and it should not have been hidden from parents for political purposes.

I had to flag this for someone in the press. My first thought was *The Daily Wire*'s Luke Rosiak. When Matt Walsh had come to Loudoun County, he brought up in his speech the sexual assault of the Smith girl. Because they both worked at *The Daily Wire* and Luke had done great work reporting on Loudoun, he seemed to be the perfect fit.

When I called him and told him, he said that he had been working on a story about the Smith family that was going to drop after the boy was convicted, but that if the name checked out with the Smiths, he would immediately write it up. I called the mom who had flagged it for me, got the name, and gave it to Luke, and he was able to confirm. He told me he had clearance from the Smiths to report it. At first, he was targeting Friday, but then told me it wouldn't be until Wednesday of the next week.

DETROIT ROCK CITY

On that Monday, I got on a flight to Seattle with a layover in Detroit. Coincidentally, I had recently rediscovered the song "Detroit Rock City" by Kiss and was listening to it repeatedly because my kids loved it. As I landed *in* Detroit and hit play on another round of my new favorite song, I checked my phone for service and logged into Twitter. Luke had already posted the story! Damn. I mean, I was glad that the story had come out, but I was sitting there on a layover in Detroit, so I couldn't exactly manage the larger message around a bombshell story that also needed to be handled with delicacy and precision because of its sensitive nature.

By the time I got to Seattle, the story was going viral. Requests for Loudoun parents to go on television and the radio were coming in fast and furiously. And I was on Pacific time, which had me completely off-kilter!

Nevertheless, by Tuesday morning, I was sitting in my hotel room talking to our team, explaining the full situation to reporters, and trying to understand all the variables at play.

To be clear, this was not a game, but it could not be ignored or left alone. There was a delicate balance. The sensitivity of the issue ordinarily required not politicizing it, but at the same time the horrific situation existed because of politics. Two young girls were sexually assaulted. One of those sexual assaults was covered up for political purposes. The other one happened because Loudoun

County Public Schools failed to do what was necessary to keep the assailant out of school while being prosecuted. This had to be handled carefully, but it had to be handled. These could be anyone's children, and it could happen again unless we exposed the rot at the core of Loudoun County Public Schools and its school board. It would require being delicate and respectful to the victims in our messaging, but it also required an aggressive push to hold them accountable, and that meant not letting Superintendent Ziegler and the school board escape their callous disregard for the safety of our children.

THE TWIST, PART I

This story just happened to have broken the night before the October 12 school board meeting in which the board would make the interim selection to replace the late Leslee King, who had passed away in August. This appointment would serve as a school board member until a special election could be held in 2022. The Democrats had gone all in for a woman named Katrece Nolen, who was fully on board with the NAACP, the equity initiatives, and critical race theory. It would make the board even worse than ever. We had convinced Paul Chen to put his name in to have a conservative balance out the possible selections. Other conservatives had applied but Fight for Schools endorsed Paul to help create a Fight for Schools versus radical leftist dynamic.

We knew Paul wouldn't get picked, but there was a solid centrist candidate named Andrew Hoyler who had run for the board against King in 2019. He was well liked and respected by a broad swath of the community and had the best shot outside of Nolen.

Our strategy was to not endorse him to give him the chance to win some Democratic support and, when he wasn't picked, blast the board for choosing a radical over a centrist candidate who everyone could live with. If he did get picked, that would mean that five school board members would do the right thing, avoid political labels, and pick someone who had support from both sides of the political divide. It would also mean that the most Democrat-leaning district in Loudoun would have a centrist representative on the school board. We could absolutely live with that.

But with six Democrats outnumbering two Republicans, there was no way Hoyler would be picked.

Except that he was.

Sitting in my hotel room, I turned on the school board meeting on my laptop. All eight school board members came out to the dais after having met to make the selection behind closed doors. Democrat Ian Serotkin formally nominated Andrew Hoyler, which was seconded by... Beth Barts. Before the vote, radical activist and Chairwoman Brenda Sheridan and political climber and Vice Chairwoman Atoosa Reaser made a substitute motion to nominate the Democrat-endorsed pick, Katrece Nolen. This was highly irregular, as usually these appointments were decided behind closed doors and voted on unanimously in public. But Sheridan and Reaser wanted to prove their unwavering fealty to the social justice warriors and the local Democrat machine. It was of no matter—five members of the board (including three Democrats) voted against the maneuver, and Hoyler was appointed to the school board.

I had heard rumors before the vote that Barts and Corbo, both Democrats, were none too happy about getting lobbied by the local

Democrat party and other high-ranking Democrat officials to cast an official vote. But I didn't expect them to actually stand strong against that kind of undue and unethical pressure. I found myself in a state of shock. There were forces at play within the school board and within the local Democrat party that I had yet to fully grasp but was beginning to understand. I suspected that Barts and, to some degree, Corbo felt betrayed and used by the local Democrat machine. That these political actors on the school board were happily letting us go head-to-head with Barts and that they hoped we would win so they could go back to engaging in their bad conduct behind closed doors once we had taken our pound of flesh.

But with this latest horrific example of malfeasance surrounding the two sexual assaults, they were in for a rude awakening.

THE TWIST, PART II

Following the vote for Hoyler, no one on the board said anything about the *Daily Wire* story, but the public commenters sure did. Person after person demanded that the smug Superintendent Ziegler resign or be fired. It was the angriest I had seen any of these parents—even after all the previous controversies.

The next day, when Ziegler finally put out a statement, it was riddled with holes. In defense of the school board, it said that school board members were not regularly informed of disciplinary matters. Well, no kidding! No one expects that the school board would be told when a kid swore in class or got in a fight at recess, but this was a sexual assault by a boy of a girl in the girls' bathroom at the same time that they were trying to pass a policy that would allow boys in girls' bathrooms.

The statement also said that the school board only became aware of specific details of the incident after the *Daily Wire* story. Reading between the lines, that clearly meant that they were aware of general details before that. Otherwise, the statement would have said that they had no awareness whatsoever.

I immediately knew what to do. We would have a press conference the next day demanding that Ziegler be fired, an independent investigation be commissioned with a report to be made public, all school board members who knew and did nothing submit their resignations, and Attorney General Garland, who was so concerned with school boards now, conduct a Title IX investigation into Loudoun County Public Schools.

When I boarded my plane on Wednesday, I put out the call to the Fight for Schools team and readied up for a 2:30 p.m. press event in front of Loudoun County Public Schools on Thursday. Getting home at 1:30 a.m. and having a fitful sleep did nothing to extinguish my fire and, in the process, help keep the anti-parent Terry McAuliffe from winning the governorship. Because if he won and Democrat Attorney General Mark Herring won reelection, this would all be swept under the rug and there would be no accountability for Ziegler and the school board and no true justice for the girls who were victimized by a school division that valued woke politics over the safety of their students.

I woke up early the next day, alerted the press to the conference, and gathered the team outside the Loudoun County Public Schools admin building, where, in front of local and national news, we hammered LCPS for its actions. We demanded the superintendent be fired, that any complicit school board members resign, that LCPS conduct an independent investigation and release its results to the public, and that Attorney General Merrick Garland investigate LCPS for Title IX violations (since he seemed to be so interested in the comings and goings at Loudoun County Public Schools).

Along with national right-of-center media, the local news was now fully covering the scandal. When I got home, I got a text from a local reporter asking me an out-of-the-blue question: "Hypothetically, what would happen if a school board member resigned after a removal petition had been filed?" I knew this was no hypothetical, but I didn't want to press. I told her the case would become moot and we would voluntarily dismiss it. I didn't get a response back.

My immediate thought was that someone was going to resign. I knew that if Beth Barts wanted to resign, now would be the time. If she messaged it right and I didn't use my bullhorn to say otherwise, she could make it clear that it was not about the recent controversy. And to be honest, Barts had been hung out to dry by the rest of the school board, particularly Brenda Sheridan and Atoosa Reaser. If there was significant knowledge and fault on the school board for the sexual assaults, it would fall to those two as leaders of the school board members who met with Ziegler regularly, not one who they didn't trust and were probably hoping would get removed.

The morning after receiving that interesting text, I was making some calls to find out where we were with our Election Day signature-gathering plan when I saw on social media that Superintendent Ziegler was holding a press conference. It was the usual drivel. He claimed he had misheard the question at the June 22 meeting and thought it was about transgender assaults in the bathroom. He also went to the tried-and-true leftist playbook and blamed Donald Trump and Betsy DeVos for their Title IX revisions, which had supposedly hamstrung the board's ability to keep a sexual predator out of school. Even a cursory reading of Title IX showed this was false.

As I was watching, I received another text from the reporter who had asked me the "hypothetical" the previous day. She simply said to stand by for major news that concerned Fight for Schools. At this point, I knew that someone was resigning, most likely Barts.

I headed to my desk to write up a statement responding to Superintendent Ziegler when my phone started buzzing off the hook with "Check Facebook. Beth Barts just quit."

Sure enough, Barts announced that she was resigning, effective on Election Day. I quickly shifted gears to write a statement on her resignation. I had to get it exactly right. On one hand, her tenure on the school board had been marked with chaos, disciplinary actions from her colleagues, and wrath from parents who had declared her enemy number one. She had also been our top target as we realized that, from a legal perspective, she would be our best case and could cause other dominoes to fall. On the other hand, while the rest of the school board members were seeking to remove themselves as victims, Barts fought back hard on her terms as her colleagues happily allowed her to be their human shield despite their engaging in the same conduct.

Our fight with Barts was over, and we were the victors. If there is one lesson I have learned in sports, politics, or life, it is this—be gracious in defeat, be even more gracious in victory. Then move on to the next challenge. This is how I communicated that:

> This could not have been an easy decision for Ms. Barts. We have
> made known our displeasure with her actions as a school board

member over the past several months, but today she has done the right thing. Her former colleagues should take notice.

The community should know, however, that the problems at Loudoun County Public Schools and on the school board go well beyond one school board member. We will continue to shine a light on Loudoun County Public Schools and will keep fighting until we have a school board of common sense, non-partisan members and a superintendent who is accountable to parents and tells the truth.

All those beliefs had turned into reality. Barts was no longer on the school board, and it was because of the school board's association with Chardonnay Antifa, woke politics, and continued failures to do the right thing when faced with a new political power: parents. Meanwhile, our efforts to accomplish this goal had turned Loudoun County into ground zero in the fight between parents and the Educational Industrial Complex, and the entire national media was now blanketing America with wall-to-wall coverage of our efforts.

Our belief that we could do all of this was vindicated, and our goals had turned into reality.

But there was one more belief I had expressed back in March that had not yet become a reality. As you may recall, I had told my fried Christy that regardless of what happened with the removal trials, the process would galvanize people so much on this issue that it might just impact the Virginia statewide elections. That wasn't necessarily a goal as it was a prediction.

By mid-October, however, that prediction was looking more

and more like it could become a reality. If Glenn Youngkin, Winsome Sears, and Jason Miyares won, it would do more to recalibrate public education than anything else we could realistically do. And if they did win, it would be due in large part to our efforts.

To make that happen, we just needed to keep going.

RULE NO. 10

DON'T LET 'EM OFF
THE ROPES

KEY LESSON: Eventually your strategies and tactics, if well executed, will bring you to a moment when you opponent is on the ropes. They've made crucial mistakes to be in that situation. When this happens, it's not time to back off. It's time to go for the knockout.

A CHAMPIONSHIP DRIVE

Yes, I like sports analogies. In this kind of competitive battle, it's helpful to stay grounded and look to similar demonstrations of strategy, tactics, and willpower that can transfer from the playing fields to the political arena. Following Beth Barts's resignation, we were on the cusp of greater things, but we needed one last championship drive to write our movement into the history books. I just needed to figure out that one final plan.

As I joined in the celebration at Jessica Mendez's house with our team on the evening that Barts resigned, I stepped aside and sat down alone to think. My first question was to better understand why Barts resigned. She would later cite threats made to her and her family as the reason, and I have no doubt that contributed. After every flare-up involving the school board that resulted in national news, people from all over the country would email some of the nastiest, most despicable things to school board members. I had seen these emails in responses to Freedom of Information Act requests following the first story about the "Anti-Racist Parents of Loudoun County," again after Tanner Cross was suspended, and then once more following the vote to shut down the June 22 school board meeting. The people sending these emails were no better than Chardonnay Antifa as far as I was concerned, and I made every effort in interviews to denounce this kind of activity.

But the fact that Fight for Schools disqualified Soros-backed Commonwealth Attorney Buta Biberaj and was allowed to be an intervening party in the case demonstrated to Barts and her lawyer that we had a good shot of winning at trial. Especially when Judge Irby appointed a new Commonwealth Attorney to try the case alongside Fight for Schools. The word I received about this person was that he was the antithesis of a Soros prosecutor and would go where the facts and the law took him.

Yet I couldn't help but wondering if there was another reason Barts resigned—she was not going to let herself be the scapegoat for Loudoun County Public Schools' culpability in covering up a sexual assault, which directly led to a second sexual assault. She was sick of being the only one to face the music when her colleagues were just as complicit, albeit less outspoken. I believed that she was stepping out of the line of fire so that the truth about the rest of the school board and administration would be open to the kind of scrutiny that wouldn't occur if they could still use Barts as their shield.

Certainly, Fight for Schools would be more than happy to move on from Barts and take the fight to the remaining four school board members, but I recognized a big problem. Barts stepping down seemed to close the book on the "Anti-Racist Parents of Loudoun County." The activities of the members of that group, while heinous and despicable, were small potatoes compared to the very real pain and trauma that were caused by Loudoun County Public Schools putting woke political agendas over student safety. Further, with the Barts case now moot, there would be no discovery, no depositions, no cross-examinations in court. Our opportunity to learn whether the "Anti-Racist Parents of Loudoun County" was sanctioned and encouraged by members of the school board and perhaps other elected officials was now over.

What we did have, however, was an opportunity to hold the school board accountable for their actions and inactions as they related to the sexual assault of the Smith's daughter. They had sat back and watched Superintendent Ziegler mislead an entire community by falsely stating that there were not records of assaults in LCPS bathrooms. Then LCPS failed to do a required Title IX investigation and did not discipline the student, and when he was released from custody after he was charged over the summer, he was allowed to roam the hallways of a new school while wearing an ankle bracelet, ultimately committing a second sexual assault.

Based on that, I came up with a new plan. Brenda Sheridan and Atoosa Reaser, as chair and vice chair, would have met with Superintendent Ziegler frequently. If anyone knew or should have known about the situation on the school board, it would have been them. Coincidentally, those were the only petitions that we had not completed yet, though with another week at early voting we would be able to wrap them up. What if we drafted new petitions that added all that had happened since the first petitions were drafted in May? What if we added to the petition Sheridan's and Reaser's presence in the "Anti-Racist Parents of Loudoun County" group while the activists plotted to keep Tanner Cross on suspension, how they shut down public comment in violation of the law, and how they did nothing to keep someone accused of sexual assault out of school while he was being prosecuted for his crime?

If we did this, it would require a massive effort from the team. It would take some time to redraft the petitions and get them into circulation, leaving only about two weeks of early voting and Election Day to get around 3,000 total signatures. Yet, if we could execute that plan, it would keep enthusiasm and energy high, and with the media descending on Loudoun County voting locations, we would be there to continue to amplify the message with a full-throated support of Glenn Youngkin's candidacy.

I worked with my lawyers to draft the new petitions and then made the ask of my core volunteers: Amy Jahr, Emily Emshwiller, Erin Smith, Erin Dunbar, Carri Michon, Erin Brown, Michele Mege, Abbie Platt, Suzanne Satterfield, and Jessica Mendez. Unsurprisingly, they were 100 percent ready to finish the game in style, and we started collecting signatures for the new petitions on October 20, giving us 13 days to finish.

After two days of collecting signatures on these new petitions, however, another bombshell dropped. I was at a bed-and-breakfast known as Zion Springs to be interviewed by Ben Domenech of *The Federalist* on what had been going on in Loudoun County. The owner, Jon Tigges, was the man arrested at the June 22 meeting for trespass, and he put together weekly meetings at Zion Springs in western Loudoun that I would occasionally attend.

I had just finished my interview with Ben and was getting ready to go home when a new story popped up on my Twitter timeline. Neal Augenstein of WTOP in Washington, D.C., reported that he had acquired an email from Superintendent Ziegler to the whole school board on the day the Smiths' daughter was sexually assaulted, informing them of the situation. THEY KNEW! All of them. Democrat, Republican, it didn't matter. The only one on that school board who wasn't culpable was Andrew Hoyler because he had only just joined. The whole board was culpable in the lie that was told to the community by Ziegler at the June 22 meeting.

In hindsight, I should have changed the petitions for Sheridan and Reaser again to include the fact that they knew and did nothing to correct the misinformation peddled by Ziegler. But we had already been working at the revisions for two days, and the train had left the station.

As we were making headway every day at early voting, a new group called Loudoun4All started showing up and passing out to voters amateurish flyers replete with factual inaccuracies, spelling mistakes, and piss-poor grammar. They were very aggressive, which turned people off and only helped us out. It also didn't help that Board of Supervisors member Juli Briskman (the one who had won her seat off the "fame" of flipping off President Trump as he drove to Trump National Golf Course in Loudoun County back in 2017[1]) was joining them in their efforts to harass the moms who were volunteering for our efforts and the people who were signing the petitions.

These zealots also seemed to have zero clue that we were circulating new petitions despite standing 10 feet away as we talked to signers. If this worked, we were going to be able to spring a massive surprise on the school board after the election.

We were smelling a whole new level of fear. This was no longer about the school board. They knew, as did we, that our efforts were having a major impact on the elections. The Friday before Election Day, we got some insight into why—polls showed Youngkin up on McAuliffe anywhere from two to eight points, with education now being the number one issue for voters.

He was going to win, and it was going to be in no small part due to our herculean efforts since March.

VICTORY

On the night before the election, Glenn Youngkin held his final rally of the campaign at the Loudoun County Fairgrounds. For months, Youngkin's rallies had been drawing massive crowds. People came from all over Virginia to hear him speak. In all my years working for political campaigns, I had never seen anything like it.

For the most part, the crowds were concerned about education. The lines about parents having the right to choose what their children were being taught in schools always drew twice the applause that anything else did. Even in the mainstream media, which had become particularly interested in the race, there were predictions that Youngkin had the race locked up. They knew that this one issue had grown beyond their ability to shut it down or control it, and that was making them panic.

By the time the night arrived, we were around 30 percent of the way to where we needed to be with our new petitions and knew that we could finish on Election Day. I tasked Suzanne Satterfield with our E-Day operation. Suzanne was a talkative mom who was also a relentless Energizer bunny; I knew she would deliver. We spent countless hours before the election planning the operation and eventual picked five locations in Sterling and five locations in Algonkian that traditionally had the most voting traffic. We would have fifty volunteers, many of them new, rotating three shifts from 6:00 a.m. to 7:00 p.m. to collect as many signatures as possible.

Our last early voting day was the Saturday before Halloween came, and I went home and prepared to have one night of relaxation at the annual Halloween party. I couldn't help but think of the Brett Kavanaugh talk with Ashley at this same party in 2018 and how it had set off a chain of events that would lead me to this crazy adventure in which I found myself at the center.

The next two days before Election Day were a whirlwind. I must have done at least 10 different media hits on television, radio, and podcast. If it weren't for a steady diet of Red Bull, I'm not sure I could have gotten through it! But the energy was there, the feeling of victory was in the air, and we were going to have to get through the next few days on adrenaline.

Then, before we knew it, it was the night before the election, and in addition to making sure everything was set for our petition-gathering operation the next day, I had to prepare to speak at Youngkin's final rally at the Loudoun County Fairgrounds in Leesburg.

As I watched the cars pull up for the rally—many of which turned around because the place was so crowded—I was nervous. I had agreed to speak before Youngkin went up and get everyone riled up to hear from him. I was used to speaking on television but never live and in front of this many people.

For the past few days, I was working on the closing statement of my life that I would deliver in front of thousands of people. This wasn't going to be about critical race theory, transgender bathrooms, or sexual assault coverups. This was going to be about how the parents in Loudoun County inspired millions to rise up and fight for their children. It would be about the parents who had lit the fire that had spread throughout Loudoun County, throughout the Commonwealth of Virginia, and throughout the United States of America. I would pull on everything I had learned and experienced and show everyone just how heroic they all were for fighting the fight of their lives. Would this speech swing any votes? No. Everyone there was going to vote for Youngkin. But if I could contribute to the growing energy and excitement to help motivate the crowd and those watching on the livestream, I was going to give it everything I had.

I was also going to have fun with it. I went back through every heroic movie I could think of that inspired me as either a kid or an adult: Rocky movies, *Hoosiers*, Marvel movies, the Dark Knight trilogy. Then I rewatched some of those old Tom Brady pre–Super Bowl speeches. I even read some passages from Joseph Campbell's "A Hero with a Thousand Faces." From there, I weaved together what I thought was the best speech I could give that reflected the heroism of the thousands of people who started a national movement right here in Loudoun County.

As I stepped up to the podium, I saw that my wife Elsie and my daughters Ava and Caroline had gotten through the traffic and made it to the corner of the bleachers that contained a large contingent of the Fight for Schools team. This made me put a little extra rocket sauce on my performance, and I was ready to light the fire of all fires under this crowd. Here it is:

Thank you very much. But I want you all to cheer for each other right now because you have inspired millions.

The politics of this country have become so divisive over the past decade or so. The politics of division, where everybody gets put into a different box and they use that to slice and dice and divide to win elections.

And then they've added the thing where it's—if you don't agree with us and have a different perspective, we're gonna cancel you.

To fight back against that you need three things. First, you need something that will unify people. Something that transcends all divisions, whether its political ideology, gender, race, ethnicity, religion. And that issue is our children.

Next, you need moms and dad that have the courage to go out there and fight for their kids. And in Loudoun County we have thousands of moms and dads that are fighting for their kids.

And we started this I said we were going to fight for our kids all day every day, and I meant all day every day!

These parents have put on a suit of armor and they have fought back. They have taken slings and arrows from elected officials, from the media, from intolerant neighbors, from the Attorney General of the United States.

But we're still here and we're not going anywhere.

The third thing that you need is a leader who can harness this movement. Someone that can give voice to parents and speak for them and stand up for them. And there are two people applying for this job of leader right now. In one corner, you have Terry McAuliffe. Terry McAuliffe thinks you're all conspiracy theorists and that he knows more about what's going on in your children's schools that you do. He gets it from Randi Weingarten and Joe Biden, they tell him what's going on so I guess that's enough.

In the other corner you have Glenn Youngkin. Glenn was extremely successful and had no reason to run for governor other than to make the Commonwealth of Virginia the best place that it can be. He has been listening to parents for months and speaking on our behalf, and if he is elected governor he is going to work for parents to have the best schools in the country.

So the question here is are you going to go with Terry McAuliffe the political servant, or Glenn Youngkin the public servant.

Now, I've been working in and observing campaigns for ten years now and I've developed an instinctive feel to know how things are going to go. Usually I can figure it out by the Friday before the election. But if I tell you what happens, it won't happen. So instead I'm going to tell you how to make it happen.

We need to go out there and get every single vote. Get every person to the polls. Hand out every sample ballot and if your collecting signatures for the school board recall, let's get every signature.

Look, I've heard a lot about this "McAuliffe machine," but I've been out at the polls and I don't see a machine. I just see people, just like us. They may be on the ropes right now, but they're still going to do their best. So it comes down to one thing—who wants it more? Do they want it more? Or do we want it more?

When I look out here, and I look across Virginia, I see heroes with thousands of faces standing up for their children.

But tomorrow, we've got to get it done.

I wasn't done yet; there was one more line to go that I hoped would make people run through a wall to win this election. Standing on that giant riser with thousands in attendance and cheering, especially my wife and children, I really did feel like we were a team of heroes. It gave me the confidence to not only say what I wanted to say but pause at the right moments, drive up the energy, enjoy it, and finish with this line: "Tomorrow, when that alarm goes off, we need to rise, suit up, and LET'S GO GET IT!"

Quite frankly, I don't know that I will ever feel that much adrenaline again in my life. I stepped off that riser and knew that Youngkin was going to win. We stayed through the cold and listened to the other speakers and watched as Youngkin's bus came through, blaring AC/DC's "Thunderstruck" as he, Winsome Sears, and Jason Miyares exited the bus.

Youngkin electrified the crowd full of parents and kids, all of whom went home cold but warmed by the potential for a massive change.

FINISH THE GAME

I drove home, immediately ate something for the first time all day, and then went to try to get three to four hours of sleep before waking up at 3:30 a.m. to head to my first shift at an Algonkian voting location. For some reason, my partner volunteer didn't make it, so it was just me for the 6:00 to 10:00 a.m. shift. About two hours in, Michele Mege came to help, and together we collected close to 200 signatures on the new Reaser petitions. If we did that in one location during one shift, we were going to finish this well before the polls closed. Once our relief team ended, I pulled off shifts and just went into command mode, driving back and forth to other locations.

Signatures were coming in by the droves. Republicans were signing, Independents were signing, Democrats were signing. The latter group would often say to our volunteers that they were voting for a Republican for the first time because they were appalled at what was going on with the schools.

I kept getting up-to-the-hour counts from Jessica, and by 4:00 p.m. we were over 125 percent of where we needed to be. I didn't spread the news quite yet—with two more hours, we could be at 150 percent and be ironclad against any challenges to the signatures in court. But I was going to call it at 6:00 p.m. so people could get home, eat dinner, and get to Youngkin's election-watching party in Fairfax.

I also had to get home to do a quick television hit on the election with *Special Report* on Fox News, but not before I returned to the polling location where I had started the day at 5:50 a.m. I went back to talk with Matt Taibbi, who was in town to cover the Loudoun County story. I am a huge fan of Matt's and the way that he calls balls and strikes and shuns the corporate media for the truth. His book *Hate Inc.* is one of the best pieces in the media ecosystem of today, and it was the brutal article he wrote about Robin DiAngelo's book *White Fragility* that had gotten me paying attention to critical race theory in the first place a year and a half before.

I unloaded everything I had on him, but he was particularly interested in the Equity Collaborative and the Loudoun County "equity" origin story. I couldn't have been more pleased. I never had the time to keep pushing that, but having a legit reporter like Matt digging in was going to be important in this fight.

After wrapping up, I got home as quickly as I could, said hi to my wife, kids, and parents, who had just gotten into town for the week, and then went outside to the satellite van to jump on *Special Report.*

Finished with TV hit number one, I went inside, ate a quick dinner, and got ready to go to Youngkin's election-night party in Fairfax County. As I was waiting for my wife, I was watching the results come in on television. It looked like Youngkin was doing well, but the real action was on Twitter, where election prognosticators like Dave Wasserman, Decision Desk, and others were starting to make the call that Youngkin and Sears were going to win. By the time we went to Jessica Mendez's house to Uber to the party, several of those prognosticators had made official calls for Youngkin and Sears.

Youngkin was getting big margins all throughout the state, and in Northern Virginia, he was outperforming where he needed to be to win. In short, barring something crazy, this was a done deal before we even got to the party.

As we walked in, I saw Paul Chen and Joe Mobley, who had both been instrumental in this now-eight-month battle. Paul was nervous, and I told him, "Relax. It's over. Youngkin won, Sears won, Miyares we'll see." He was dubious, but I was sure. We went up to the main ballroom and started mingling with the crowd before I had to go outside and do a hit on *The Ingraham Angle* along with Asra Nomani, one of the amazing leaders of the Fairfax parents, who had become a close ally.

After doing about 10 minutes with Laura and being completely and utterly exhausted, I was able to go back in and fully enjoy this moment with the Fight for Schools team. We waited and waited for Youngkin to come out, but right before he did, the PA system started playing Youngkin's go-to again: "Thunderstruck." In a moment that I will never forget, all of us put our arms around each other's shoulders and started jumping and yelling in unison, "All day every day, all day every day, all day every day." We captured that on video, and I tweeted, "So you're probably wondering how I got here." Withing a few hours, that tweet had gone viral, symbolizing how everyday parents had changed the course of political history in Virginia and beyond.

I had a moment while we were waiting of tearing up a bit. What we had just accomplished was a political thunderclap. Parents had risen up to fight for their kids against a school system that had been captured by politics. I may have been a key player in that, but I was just in the right place at the right time to help lead the fight. Everyone had done what it took to fight, and something we hadn't even planned—winning what eight months earlier seemed like an unwinnable election—had become reality. We had been the catalysts for change. Not some big money organization. Not a political party apparatus. We had driven our message and our concerns upstream through action, and Youngkin, Sears, and Miyares had done what great candidates do—they had listened to the people and made their campaigns about those people.

Winsome Sears spoke first and, as always, delivered a dynamite speech. Here we were: a Black woman from Haiti who was also a Marine Corps veteran was the first women of color to hold statewide office—and as a Republican, no less. Youngkin followed her and once more fired up the crowd of parents who had given so much to make change and had been rewarded beyond their wildest imaginations.

In a moment of weakness, I decided I had to send a shot across the bow to all the woke keyboard warriors in Loudoun County who had called us all racists, fascist, and transphobes and had plotted against us back in March and beyond. I had generally never engaged with these sad humans on social media, but tonight was different. Naming some of the more prominent members of Chardonnay Antifa on Twitter, I thanked them for the massive role that they had in the election and said with satisfaction: "Have a drink on me." In hindsight, this was a mistake. I should have said: "Have a Chardonnay on me!"

RULE NO. 11

DON'T BE OVERLY RELIANT ON PAST SUCCESS

KEY LESSON: The greater the success, the greater the dangers that follow. Complacency will often set in as will the tendency to overly rely on the strategies and tactics that brought victory. Eventually your opponents will adapt to your tendencies and will exploit any signs of arrogance, impatience, and repetition.

EUPHORIA

In the weeks following the election, everyone on our team was shell-shocked. There's a special kind of feeling you get when months and months of work pay off. There's nothing else in the world like it.

During the weeks that followed, I would often tell people that they had been part of a true inflection point in American politics and that it would be tough, if not impossible, to ever match the shocking impact of moms and dads coming together to effectuate change in Virginia and throughout the American political land-scape like we had all done.

Even though I had been in the middle of political battles for over 10 years, the Fight for Schools saga had catapulted me into the public eye in a way that I never would have expected. It didn't matter what I did in the future. Nothing was going to top what had just occurred over the course of a single year in Loudoun County, Virginia.

But our mission had never been about winning an election, even if we knew that it was a by-product of our fight. But that is exactly what Chardonnay Antifa was spouting off about on social media and a narrative that some in the media were pushing. So it was always in the back of my mind that we would prove them wrong by continuing to file our removal cases even after the election.

We had just finished off two brand-new removal petitions in 13 days, and we were impatient to prove them wrong. Further, since we had already been successful with our legal strategy against Barts, we would just rinse and repeat and get the same result. There was no way we were going to wait to file the removal petitions against Brenda Sheridan and Atoosa Reaser when we smelled more victory just around the corner. We were confident, we would be aggressive, and we would repeat our model of success.

But this time, the empire would strike back.

WE ARE NOW IN COURT

Even before we finished collecting signatures for Sheridan and Reaser on Election Day, I had it in my mind that we would file against Sheridan at the following Tuesday's school board meeting, regardless of whether Youngkin or McAuliffe won.

But after Youngkin won, I started to have doubts about filing right away. Both Youngkin and now Attorney General-elect

Jason Miyares had pledged to investigate Loudoun County Public Schools for the way it handled the sexual assaults in May and October. That investigation would only begin after they were inaugurated, and who knew how long it would take. But if we waited to file the removals until after the results, we could have more information that would help our cases. On the other hand, we had just worked our tails off finishing those two petitions in 13 days, and we would lose momentum and interest if we waited. I decided that it would be better to take our shots now, and even if things didn't go our way, we'd still have the chance at justice and accountability from the new attorney general's investigation. While a removal trial was only quasi-criminal, an attorney general investigation was *very* criminal.

Having made up my mind, on November 9 I drove down to the Loudoun County Courthouse in Leesburg and filed the petition for the removal of Brenda Sheridan right at 3:30 p.m. The reason I made sure to file at such an odd time had to do with the element of surprise. At the time, almost no one knew that we were about to file to have Sheridan removed, and I wanted to keep it that way. I knew that if I submitted the paperwork just before the court closed at 4:00 p.m., the petition would officially be filed, but it would not be in the electronic system yet and, thus, less likely to be discovered and leaked before we could announce it on our terms.

On my way back from the courthouse, I emailed a press release and the petition to several reporters who had been following and covering the Loudoun County saga. I explained that it was embargoed until I emailed them back to lift the embargo, meaning that in exchange for me giving them the information early, they could write their stories but could not publish until I gave permission. In this case, I would do that only after my school board speech.

By the time I was done priming the press pump, the school board meeting was set to begin. I pulled into the parking lot a few minutes before it began and got on the line of people waiting to speak. Once again, the line was long, but this time we weren't sweating but rather freezing. No matter how many times I attended one of these school board meetings, I still found it slightly hard to believe that *this* many people wanted to make their voices heard at such a small, locally focused meeting. And it wasn't only the speakers.

Outside, there was a small rally of people who'd set up a television screen so they could watch the meeting as it was happening. Whoever was speaking would effectively be performing to this overflow crowd outside. If Loudoun County school board meetings were to become sleepy affairs once more, tonight would not be the night where that would happen.

As I waited in line to sign up, I thought about my last speech before the school board, which had occurred on October 26. I intentionally signed up to speak last and once more opted against attempting for a TV moment but rather telegraphed what I knew we were going to do after the election. On that night, I said:

> I can't believe I'm about to say this, but a week and a half ago a member of this school board stepped up, made the hard choice, and did the right thing. And now, you don't have your human shield to take the slings and arrows. So the spotlight of accountability turns to you. And nowhere does that spotlight burn brighter than you Chairwoman Sheridan. You are the leader of this school board, you have been for two years. You have overseen the worst public body in the country, and the buck stops

with you. You knew when Superintendent Ziegler got up there and lied—that wasn't a misunderstanding—and you said nothing. And you did nothing to keep the kid out of school. I know you all think that we're done with Ms. Barts so we're done. But here's the message: the truth will come out, justice will prevail, AND WE WILL SEE YOU IN COURT.

At the time, I'm sure they assumed this was just an empty threat. I'm sure they didn't really believe I was going to file another case. In the eyes of the school board, Fight for Schools was just a group of aggrieved parents who wanted to stick it to a few people who tried to cancel them on Facebook. They believed that we had gotten together out of anger and that the influence we held over the state's gubernatorial election had gone to our heads. Now that our preferred candidate was headed for the governor's mansion and Beth Barts was off the school board, I'm sure they thought we were going to fade away and disband.

That wasn't going to happen—by now they should have realized that when I said we were going to do something, we did it.

When it was my turn to speak on November 9, I tore into the school board once again. I wasn't able to position myself as the final speaker, but as the next-to-last speaker, I provided a book-end for my comment in late October: "I told you this wasn't about an election. We're still here. Here with a petition for the removal of Chairwoman Sheridan; and it's not the old petition, this is a new petition. Drafted about two and a half weeks ago and completed in thirteen days with 1,200 signatures. This petition has on it things like: violating the First Amendment of speakers and listeners in this boardroom, remaining in the private Facebook group while people were plotting a disruption at Leesburg elementary to keep Tanner Cross on administrative leave, and doing nothing and allowing a now convicted sex offender to go to a different school where he then committed another alleged sexual assault."

Then, just when they thought I was going to leave, I dropped the hammer.

"I said we'd see you in court," I said, "As of 3:30 today, WE ARE NOW IN COURT."

The applause erupted outside as soon as I was done speaking. Walking out of the room, I thought about what it must have felt like to be one of the school board members, knowing that Fight for Schools was not just a one-time inconvenience. We were a group that was going to hold them accountable for wrongdoing regardless of timing, politics, or convenience.

And we were not done yet.

A few weeks later, I repeated the process for Atoosa Reaser. Jessica Mendez drove to the courthouse, filed at 3:55, and came to a fundraiser we were holding at Sharon Virts's home, Selma Mansion. This time, I gave a speech to the packed room of donors, and at the end of the speech, I announced that we had just filed on Reaser. With $50K raised that night, we certainly gave our fantastic supporters their money's worth.

Since the rally was held just a few weeks after the election, everyone was still on a high. We also had a great lineup of speakers: Winsome Sears opened the event virtually from Richmond, where she was getting ready to take office in January. Asra Nomani, who had been the key parent organizer in neighboring Fairfax County, spoke next and highlighted the accomplishments of parents all over Virginia before introducing me. When it was my turn to speak, I thanked everyone for their hard work and summed up our progress so far. Near the end, I reminded them again of how far we had come—and how much everyone had doubted us along the way.

"In the summer," I said, "they didn't think we were going to get the signatures for Beth Barts. Then, when we did, they said she would never resign, and then she did. They said that after that, we would be done, and that we weren't going after everyone else. Last week, we showed them otherwise when we filed our removal petitions against Chairwoman Brenda Sheridan. Today, we reminded them again—at 3:55 p.m. we filed petitions containing over 1,800 signatures to remove Vice Chair Atoosa Reaser."

For the rest of the night, I stuck around and spoke with our volunteers. The glow of the election had not worn off, and people stayed late into the night reveling in the change that was coming to Virginia and seemed to be sweeping the country.

CHARDONNAY ANTIFA, INC.

As we began preparing for legal proceedings, we did notice that resistance to our message was a little more robust than usual. Most of it, I realized, was coming from a group called Loudoun for All. At its highest aspiration, this group was supposed to be a neutral entity that fact-checked political rhetoric in the state of Virginia. They were supposed to stand up for parents and administrators and everyone who had a stake in our education system. In reality, they were just another group of bullies who couldn't stand the fact that their side was losing. In time, I started to call them Chardonnay Antifa, Inc.

The tactics were the same. Whenever we held a rally, they would release a sheet that claimed to "fact check" every word we were saying. When we were collecting signatures for Sheridan and Reaser, they would pass out "fact checking" sheets to people leaving polling places. These "fact checks" were replete with nothing more than conclusions with no actual facts, but they did have their fair share of typos and grammatical errors. In the narrative they were pushing to readers, Fight for Schools was a bunch of crazy thugs who did nothing all day but send horrid threats to school board members.

Now, a word on threats and inappropriate messages: I'm not saying that they don't exist. As I said earlier, in various FOIA productions, I had seen some pretty egregious emails sent to school board members after various flare-ups that went national—the "Anti-Racist Parents of Loudoun County" fiasco, the Tanner Cross suspension, and the sexual assault cover-up. To that end, I tried to weave into my messaging that these kinds of communications were completely inappropriate and unhelpful. Granted, the overwhelming majority of these were not legitimate threats and were likely coming from outside Loudoun County, but I consistently went out of my way to denounce this behavior. I held a press conference the day before the June 22 school board meeting in which I told people to speak with substance on the issues. I told *The Washington Post* that we denounced all egregiously inappropriate emails and communications to school board members. I repeatedly echoed that message during television and radio interviews. When one of our volunteers sent a nonthreatening but inappropriate message to one of the school board members, I told him he needed to apologize (which he did) and emailed the school board member to let her know that the message was unacceptable.

But Loudoun for All wasn't concerned about the facts and

evidence. Once they found a "threat," they would associate it with me and Fight for Schools, without any factual basis, and use it to paint our entire organization in a bad light. Often, they did it during interviews with local television stations, which had been covering the education wars of Loudoun County for months.

After a while, I had seen enough from these amateurs and decided to engage. Specifically, in the first school board meeting after Thanksgiving, I noticed that our numbers at school board meetings were getting smaller while the numbers of people who'd come to support Loudoun for All were getting bigger. In the early days, we would usually outnumber the school board apologists about eight to two. At this meeting, however, it was more like 50-50. Granted, I had been on vacation as had others, so it could have simply been people dealing with busy schedules, but I also suspected that there was complacency setting in.

But I didn't think the answer to this small organization was more fighting. After the events of the past year, we were on top of the world and had acquired enough political capital that we could either ignore them or engage them from a position of strength. This was my mindset when Loudoun for All amateurishly thumped its chest about media coverage on Twitter with this: "Check out our media coverage from the School Board meeting yesterday. #Loudoun-County #Loudoun4All #TruthMatters #ElectionsNotRecalls."

I decided to test their seriousness as an organization by tweeting this message back to them:

"How about this Loudoun4All? I'll hear you out, you hear me out. But we will discuss your false claims of 'misinformation' 'baseless recalls' and 'outside forces.' #loudouncounty"

Within days, they reached out and told me that they would take me up on the offer. I was actually excited for the opportunity. Finally, someone was willing to sit down and have a conversation in good faith.

Later that week I met with Tom and Rebecca from Loudoun for All at Barnes & Noble. But first, they wanted me to agree to one rule—they needed to record the meeting. It struck me as paranoia on their part and slightly funny, but if that made them feel like they were in a warm and fuzzy safe space, then so be it.

But once things got going, I took an immediate liking to Tom. He was complimentary to what we had been able to accomplish, and he was grateful that I had been willing to have a conversation with them. We even went off on a tangent about football, which definitely showed me that he was a normal guy who wasn't as radicalized as some may have assumed.

As they continued to harp on the "threats" to school board members, I reminded them that I had always told members of my group to keep things civil. We were arguing about politics and professional conduct; anything personal did not belong in the conversation.

In the end, we agreed to send a message together to stop the personal attacks from all sides. They asked if I would be willing to do a joint statement, and I immediately said yes. We even came up with a press release that included the names of both our groups. When it went out, the response was mostly positive. People from all over the county commented to let us know how refreshing it was to see two rival groups coming together and agreeing that in spite of our differences, we could still have civil conversations with one another.

But it didn't last long.

Shortly after releasing the statement, our local NBC affiliate reached out to Tom and me to interview us about the statement. We both agreed. I talked about how this was a good opportunity to demonstrate that, while our groups may disagree on the issues, we can agree on how to conduct ourselves with respect to those debates. When I watched the story on television later that night, I saw Tom being interviewed by a journalist. Asked whether Fight for Schools sent threatening emails, he replied, "Let's just say there have been threats."

Obviously, these people had no sense of honor. I had reached out to Loudoun for All. I had agreed to do a statement to add to the multitude of times I had already said what the joint statement would communicate. Yet when they had the chance to make it clear that threats were not coming from Fight for Schools, Tom buckled under the pressure and had to take a shot.

Yes, I knew that this could happen. That they wanted to use me to elevate themselves and get on our level with the media. But honestly, I didn't care. They were unprofessional and clueless, and I didn't think they'd become much more than a social media account with maybe a few thousand followers if that. More importantly, I gave Fight for Schools and its supporters the moral high ground that they had earned.

Then I put it all in the back of my mind. For now, we had work to do.

HEADING TO ANOTHER VICTORY...

In early January, we were once more at the Loudoun County Circuit Court for motion hearings in the Sheridan and Reaser cases, which would be heard at the same time. Once more, we were arguing against a motion to dismiss, for the disqualification of Commonwealth Attorney Buta Biberaj, and for Fight for Schools to be allowed to be part of the case as an intervenor.

This time, however, it was not only Fight for Schools supporters in the courtroom. Now that local Democrat party favorite Atoosa Reaser was on the hot seat, the local party faithful started showing up in a way that they hadn't done for Barts. We still outnumbered them, but it was clear that they were now ready to join the fight.

As we had in the Barts case, we had Judge Irby and were pleased that someone who clearly knew what was going on would be overseeing the case. Once more, I had to testify to establish the reasons why Fight for Schools should intervene and why Biberaj should be booted from the proceedings. In the Barts case, Biberaj cross-examined me for maybe 10 minutes. This time, it would be closer to two hours. I had been a royal pain in the side of Biberaj and other far-left Democrats in Loudoun, and she wanted her pound of flesh.

For months, we had been watching Biberaj at work—or, as was more often the case, *not* work. In November 2019, she was elected with the help of about $659,000 in money from a PAC associated with George Soros. It was well known around the country that Soros and his cronies had been attempting to install local law enforcement officials who would implement a leftist agenda that was more focused on social justice than fixing crime. Biberaj was a prime example—her social media feeds were brazenly political for what is supposed to be a neutral prosecutor, and she'd come under fire for engaging in soft-on-crime policies and decisions that had disastrous consequences.[1]

During that time, she had also refused to speak to the press and made very few public statements. I often found myself wondering what the woman behind the curtain was actually like.

On the stand during trial, I found out. I wasn't impressed.

As a young lawyer, you learn that when you're cross-examining someone, it should effectively be *you* making your point, not them. Even though they're the ones answering the questions, you should be absolutely certain of what the answers are going to be before you ask your questions. That's Lawyering 101, and you can learn it just by watching *A Few Good Men*. Biberaj did the opposite.

Getting cross-examined by Biberaj felt like being a cornerback playing against a quarterback who looks down his receivers and throws at them when well covered. I was polite in my responses and waited for the inevitable opportunity to jump a route and take it to the house.

For example, she asked me: "Is Fight for Schools anti-equity?"

When I responded that "Fight for Schools is pro equal opportunity. Equal opportunity and equity are two different things," she tried to push back by saying I needed to answer her question as asked. So I shot back, "How do you define equity?"

When Biberaj tried to claim that she didn't have to define it, the judge said to her, "He shouldn't have to guess what you mean by it. So what do you mean by equity?"

Now I was the one who had Biberaj on defense, and she had to define it with this muddled compound question: "Within the school system equity being affording equal opportunity to the individuals that attend schools, are you anti that?"

I avoided her use of the word "equity" and simply said, "I absolutely support equal opportunity for individuals that attend schools."

I couldn't believe how incompetent she was. This was the person who was elected to be our chief prosecutor? I was starting to have fun.

She later came back with a slow, hanging curve right over the plate when she asked if membership in the "Anti-Racist Parents of Loudoun County" is "a basis by which you think it's appropriate to remove a school board member."

I had been waiting on this one and responded, "Membership in that group from a member of the Loudoun County School Board after that story broke, yes, that diminishes the public trust in those school board members that remained in those groups, saying nothing about it."

She tried to recover by saying that the trust was only diminished for "you and your board for Fight for Schools," which allowed me to slam the door shut on her line of questioning with me responding, "And the thousands of people that signed the petition."

The back-and-forth continued for what seemed like an eternity, but I was having fun with it and felt that the judge was once again seeing through Biberaj's antics.

Our attorney, Dave Warrington, and Sheridan's and Reaser's attorneys all made closing arguments, but Biberaj said she needed more time to prepare for an argument for Reaser. This made zero sense to us and to the judge, who reminded Biberaj that the cases were exactly the same, and she'd had weeks to prepare. Nevertheless, Biberaj's word salad rambling convinced the judge to give her the opportunity to submit her closing on Reaser in writing, and we would have a decision shortly thereafter.

Needless to say, I left the courtroom that day feeling pretty good. But I did have a suspicion that something was up. There was no reason for Biberaj to make herself look like an idiot in front of the judge if she didn't have a plan.

As it turned out, she did.

THE EMPIRE STRIKES BACK

A few weeks after the hearing, Biberaj all of a sudden submitted a motion to recuse herself from the Reaser case on the grounds that they were both lawyers who were members of the Loudoun County Bar Association. Really? That's why she was going to recuse? Not because there were a dozen public photos of Biberaj and Reaser at political events together? Not because Biberaj had been an active member in the "Anti-Racist Parents of Loudoun County"? Not because she personally prosecuted Scott Smith for disorderly conduct at the June 22 school board meeting and was involved in the recommendation for his daughter's assailant to return to school?[2] Those were legitimate reasons for her to recuse, as they created real conflicts of interest in these removal cases, which dealt with those very issues. Recusing because you're part of a legal social club? That felt like a setup. It felt like Buta knew she would get disqualified, so she needed to find a benign reason to recuse and then work behind the scenes to find a like-minded prosecutor to volunteer as her replacement, just like what had happened in Fairfax the summer before when their removal petitions were voluntarily dismissed by a Soros-backed prosecutor who stepped in for another Soros-backed prosecutor.[3]

Then things started to get really strange. The Loudoun NAACP, now represented by Charlie King, filed their own motion to intervene in the case, claiming that the removals were a "Jim

Crow effort of 2022 to suppress votes."[4] Meanwhile, just as word had reached us that Judge Irby was ready to issue a decision and we should schedule a date to return to court, I started hearing whispers that political machinations in Richmond were occurring and Irby was not going to be reappointed to the bench. Sure enough, she was not reappointed and recused from our case, and that was followed by every Loudoun County Circuit Court judge recusing as well. To top it off, the head of the Loudoun NAACP issued this bizarre statement, seeming to take credit for Irby having to recuse:

> She had already made up her decision to give them [Fight for Schools] standing and allow them in the case. The only thing that stopped her dead in her tracks, which she hadn't accounted for, was the intervening of the oldest civil rights organization into this case, and Judge Irby said "I'm out." She decided to save her career and work on her reappointment, versus carrying out this injustice that would have been exposed.

The Loudoun County anti-parent cartel, as I started calling them, had been completely absent for Beth Barts. They clearly wanted her gone and thought there would be no harm in letting us do the work for them. What they underestimated, of course, was that our efforts to even get into court in that case would spark a massive parents' revolution that completely shifted power in Virginia. They weren't going to make the same mistake twice and, with the aid of our old friend from the Barts case—Charlie King— they had devised a coordinated plan to spike the removals of Sheridan and Reaser.

Eventually a retired judge from Virginia Beach was appointed to the case, and his first move was to appoint the Democrat Commonwealth Attorney from Charlottesville who, conveniently, was part of the Virginia Progressive Prosecutors for Justice organization. Also in that group were Buta Biberaj, Steve Descano (the Soros-backed Fairfax Commonwealth Attorney who recused from the Fairfax removal case), and Jim Hingely (the Soros-backed Abermarle Commonwealth Attorney who took over for Descano and voluntarily dismissed the Fairfax removal cases).

The fix was in, and we knew it.

Because we had a new judge, we had to reargue our motions from January. The arguments were set for May, but the judge never took testimony. He simply read the transcripts from the January hearing. The judge denied both Fight for Schools' and the Loudoun NAACP's motions to intervene. Then he disqualified Biberaj from the Sheridan case and appointed the Charlottesville Commonwealth Attorney to prosecute that case as well as Reaser's. What did the Commonwealth Attorney do? Argued along with Sheridan and Reaser that the case should be dismissed. Having no opposition on record, the judge dismissed the removal cases against Sheridan and Reaser on May 23.

We had seen the writing on the wall, but it looked like the other side had done the writing behind closed doors. Loudoun for All showed up. The rest of the Democrats on the school board showed up. The Loudoun NAACP showed up. Almost as if they had put the wheels in motion and knew exactly how it would go down.

After the decision was handed down, I immediately left the courtroom to go speak with the media assembled outside. How one handles defeat is equally if not more important than how one handles victory. We hadn't seen a lot of defeats, so it was important to go out there and show the world that we would be gracious but that we would also continue to fight.

As I drove home, I thought to myself that we lost the removal because we had been too predictable, too impatient, and too reliant on what we had done in the past. Perhaps if we had done the harder thing and held off on filing the petitions until after Attorney General Miyares had concluded his investigation, we would have had a greater chance of success. Maybe if we had come up with a trick play into these two cases, as opposed to relying on our earlier strategy, we would have been less predictable and could have countered the opposition's game with one of our own. But at the end of the day, the removal campaign had lasted 14 months, one school had board member stepped down, and we had helped create the circumstances that helped parent-friendly candidates like Glenn Youngkin, Winsome Sears, and Jason Miyares win in November.

When I arrived back at my desk, I started crafting a statement. I tried to keep the same light tone that I had used throughout the entire process, throwing in a few pop culture references to keep the people entertained. I titled the release "Breaking: The Empire Strikes Back in Loudoun County." The way I saw it, 2021 had been like the first *Star Wars* film. We had come together and done amazing things. We'd held our school board accountable and ultimately helped elect a Republican governor in blue Virginia. Just months earlier, that might have seemed impossible, but we had blown up the Richmond Death Star. But over the past couple of months, things had taken a dark turn, not unlike *The Empire Strikes Back*. In an homage to the films of my youth, I concluded the press release with this:

We always knew that this would be a three year process to make the necessary changes in Loudoun County. In 2021, the scrappy underdog parents won a massive victory, but today the empire struck back. But as we all know, the heroes always come back in the third act to finish their business...

After the end of the text of the release, I simply included a GIF of Luke Skywalker getting his new lightsaber at the end of *Return of the Jedi*.

What Sheridan, Reaser, Biberaj, and all the rest did not realize was that, while they were all focused on the shiny object that was their removal case, we were already in the third act.

PLAY THE ENDGAME

KEY LESSON: Always know your endgame and always operate with that endgame in mind. Understand that what started as your primary goal may become subsumed into something much greater than you could have imagined. When it comes time to shift to that greater purpose, let your opponents distract themselves with what they think they know and where they think they can win while you silently redeploy your efforts to the final victory.

A NEW APPROACH

In March 2021, when we first decided to pursue the removal of the six school board members who were involved in the "Anti-Racist Parents of Loudoun County" Facebook group, we knew the odds were not in our favor outside of Beth Barts. She had already faced discipline twice from the Loudoun County School Board, and her call to action in the private Facebook group ultimately led to participants plotting to cancel other members of their community and discussions of committing cybercrimes against them. Even though

Barts herself never overtly participated in or encouraged these specific discussions, her involvement made the case against her the most likely to succeed.

The rest of the cases would be tougher, as we had no direct evidence that any of the other school board members had been actively involved with the enemies list. Because of the strange way in which the removal statute in Virginia is written, there have been no elected officials removed by that process. Several have resigned before trial, but most cases would run into the same political machinations that we did with Sheridan and Reaser. Once Barts resigned, the odds of further success diminished. We knew that we were playing with house money at that point, so we decided to try new petitions that alleged a neglect of duty by Sheridan and Reaser as it related to the sexual assaults and the school board's failure to deal honestly with the community after Superintendent Ziegler completely misled everyone at the June 22 school board meeting.

But even with those stronger petitions, the idea that lightning would strike twice in a process that has traditionally been unsuccessful was based on hope—and hope is not a strategy. Which meant we would have to rethink our approach and decide the best approach for ensuring that the Loudoun County School Board and the administration were held accountable for their actions over the previous several years. That was our endgame.

Fortunately, much of the work had been accomplished when Glenn Youngkin was elected governor and Jason Miyares was elected attorney general. A mere two days after the election, Miyares confirmed what he and Youngkin had said during the campaign—the Office of the Attorney General would open an investigation into Loudoun County Public Schools.[1]

Meanwhile, the powers that be at LCPS were in shock. Had Terry McAuliffe become governor and Mark Herring been reelected as attorney general, Loudoun County Public Schools could go back to doing whatever it was that they wanted without fear of investigation. Now the school board and Ziegler would find the full might of the law breathing down their necks. On October 28, just as the polls started showing Youngkin pulling ahead, Ziegler hired a law firm to do an "independent review" of how the school system handled the sexual assaults. Of course, they didn't announce that until November 5, three days after the election and one day after Miyares announced that his office would open an investigation after being inaugurated on January 15.[2] The timing of the announcement said more than the announcement itself— they were in self-preservation mode.

Seeing this, I knew that our efforts were now secondary to the main event and that whatever resulted from the criminal investigation, whether indictments or a blistering report, I had seen enough evidence to know that it would not end well for the school board or Superintendent Ziegler. I hadn't formulated a strategic course of action yet, but I knew that it would reveal itself in time. I also knew that whatever it was, it would not be the kind of must-see TV of the year before but would involve a death by a thousand cuts approach.

With this in mind, I showed up at the last school board meeting of the year to speak once more and offer a cryptic warning of our plans:

There will be no loss of the proverbial eye of the tiger. We have just begun to fight for our children's souls. So I will tell you this— put down *Lawn Boy*, put down *Penthouse*, whatever your jam is, and pick up Sun Tzu. I will read one passage for you: "Let your plans be dark and impenetrable as night and when you move, fall like a thunderbolt." In 2022, we will strike like a thunderbolt. We are going to outsmart you, we are going to outwork you, we are going to outcompete you, and when push comes to shove, we are going to outwill you. And on January 15, we're going to get some air support.

January 15 would be inauguration day, and immediately after taking office, Youngkin would immediately issue nine executive orders, two[3] of which were central to the fight of parents across Virginia:

Executive Order Number One delivers on his Day One promise to restore excellence in education by ending the use of divisive concepts, including Critical Race Theory, in public education.

Executive Order Number Two delivers on his Day One promise to empower Virginia parents in their children's education and upbringing by allowing parents to make decisions on whether their child wears a mask in school.

But it was his fourth executive order[4] that dealt specifically with Loudoun County Public Schools. It read:

AUTHORIZING AN INVESTIGATION OF LOUDOUN COUNTY PUBLIC SCHOOLS BY THE ATTORNEY GENERAL

By virtue of the authority vested in me as Governor, I hereby issue this Executive Order requesting the Attorney General conduct a full investigation into Loudoun County Public Schools.

IMPORTANCE OF THE ISSUE

In the Spring of 2021, the Loudoun County School Board and the administration of the Loudoun County Public Schools were made aware of a sexual assault that occurred in a Loudoun County high school. A decision was made to transfer the assailant to another Loudoun County high school, where the student was able to commit a second sexual assault. The Loudoun County School Board and school administrators withheld key details and knowingly lied to parents about the assaults.

Neither the Loudoun County School Board, nor the administrators of the Loudoun County school system, have been held accountable for deceiving the very Virginians they serve. Virginia parents deserve answers and assurances that the safety of their children will never be compromised.

ATTORNEY GENERAL AUTHORIZATION

By virtue of the authority vested in me by §2.2-511 of the Code of Virginia, I am requesting the Attorney General to initiate and coordinate investigative and prosecutorial efforts and to take such actions as he may deem appropriate in order to protect the citizens of the Commonwealth and hold accountable any individuals who have violated existing law or violated the rights of victims of crime.

EFFECTIVE DATE

This Executive Directive shall be effective upon its signing and shall remain in force and effect unless amended or rescinded by future executive order or directive.

Given under my hand and under the Seal of the Commonwealth of Virginia, this 15th day of January, 2022.

With that one order, the new mission was clear: make sure that investigators knew everything that we knew while working independently to uncover more facts to put into the public domain that could theoretically aid those investigators in bringing their case.

Fortunately, Patti Menders, who had been a key organizer throughout 2021, had been hired as a community liaison in the attorney general's office. I presumed that all the work we had done to publicly make the case—press releases, opinion pieces—would be reviewed by the attorney general's office and that in the future such publicly available materials that we would generate would also receive close scrutiny by the lawyers and investigators working on the case.

As I was working this out, I also had to decide what to do for a job! I had raised over $500,000 for Fight for Schools and never taken a penny for my efforts. I certainly didn't feel comfortable paying myself while dozens of other people were volunteering their time sitting in the heat, cold, rain, or hail collecting signatures for six months. But I had spent so much time and energy on this effort that my public relations business was starting to dry up. I didn't have the time to fully devote to my existing clients and certainly didn't have the time for new ones. To be honest, I was done taking on clients for causes that I didn't want to wake up fighting for. I had one now, and I wanted to take the lessons I had learned in 2021 and utilize them to help parents throughout the country.

It just so happened that I attended a conference put on by the group Parents Defending Education. I had gotten to know its founder Nikki Neilly, and she had done a fantastic job putting together this organization that was investigating school districts across the country, bringing different parent groups together, and creating a national model of parent activism. Also at that meeting was Gene Hamilton, a lawyer who I had worked with when he was one of the top advisors in the attorney general's office at the Department of Justice. We took some time to catch up, and he told me about America First Legal (AFL), an organization he had started with Stephen Miller, one of President Trump's key advisors.

AFL is a public interest legal organization that had successfully fought against the Biden administration's "equity" policies, such as the one that discriminated against farmers and ranchers by only providing certain benefits to those who were part of certain racial or ethnic categories. It was racist and a clear violation of federal antidiscrimination law. AFL was having none of it, brought a lawsuit against the administration, and won.

I told him that I would love to be part of the team. As a lawyer, communicator, and now someone with street cred in the parents' rights movement, I could be a utility player in securing plaintiffs to hold these woke school systems accountable in court. Over the next few weeks, we talked more, and ultimately, I joined America First Legal as a senior advisor.

One of my first missions would be to recruit parents for a lawsuit against Loudoun County Public Schools for its violation of parental rights as it related to its infusion of woke ideologies of critical race theory and gender theory into the school system. Between Tanner Cross's lawsuit, our removal cases, and the latest case on masks, I learned that there was an addition to Rule No.

2—Activate, Investigate, Communicate and LITIGATE. It was time to put that into practice.

ENCIRCLEMENT

While Loudoun County's anti-parent cartel was focused on political machinations to deal with the shiny object of the pending removal case, the parents of Loudoun County were encircling them with litigation and other creative tactics that leveraged the fact that we now had a friendly administration in Richmond.

After Governor Youngkin's executive order made masks in schools optional, Loudoun County Public Schools did what they always do—they doubled down and voted to keep masks mandatory. Three parents—Kristen Barnett, Heather Yescavage, and Colin Doninger—filed a lawsuit after LCPS started suspending children for following Youngkin's order and choosing not to wear masks in school.

Before that case could even be heard, the Virginia legislature passed a law that made masks optional in schools effective March 1, and Governor Youngkin signed the bill on February 17. I took my wife and two daughters to the signing ceremony, excited to get them to see how a bill became a law! On the way back to Loudoun, LCPS once more tried to flex its muscles by saying that it would make masks optional starting on February 23, but later that night the judge in the parents' case issued a withering decision in which he said that the mask policies of Loudoun County's school board had done "irreparable harm" to children and enjoined LCPS from requiring masks, effective immediately.[5]

At the same time as this was happening, Fight for Schools was ready to go right at Superintendent Ziegler. To fire a super-intendent, either the local school board must vote to remove him or the Virginia Board of Education, upon recommendation of the State Superintendent of Education, can remove him. With a new Youngkin-appointed state superintendent at the helm of what would soon be a Youngkin majority on the state board of education, I spent several days composing a 14-page letter detailing eight specific mis-representations that Superintendent Ziegler had made in the past 18 months. I closed the letter out by asking for the removal of Ziegler and sent the letter off to Richmond and the media.[6]

Shortly thereafter, I received correspondence back from Super-intendent Jillian Balow indicating that they were taking these alle-gations seriously and were awaiting the results of Attorney General Miyares's investigation.[7] We had planted the seed.

The next month, I received a call from a special education teacher who, along with another teacher in the class, had been touched repeatedly and inappropriately by a student dozens of times a day for over two months. When they went to the administration, they were simply told to wear an apron to prevent the student from con-tinuing to grope them. I connected the teacher with a lawyer and told her that she should consider speaking out at a school board meeting. She was reticent to do that, so I told her that I could go and speak about it. I was sure that if I brought at least some details to light publicly, the school board would freak out and actually do something. That is exactly what happened. The day after my speech, the child was moved out of the classroom. Of course, that didn't solve the problem for the next teacher, and it ultimately lead to the school starting to build a case against the teachers for speaking out, even if through a surrogate.

In April, two more parents—Megan Rafalski and Megan Clegg—had another case heard in Loudoun County Circuit Court. This case challenged the closure of the June 22 meeting as a Freedom of Information Act violation, and once more, the parents were successful, and the school board was on the hook for violating parents' rights.[8]

But the biggest shoe to drop would come later in April as the media reported that the attorney general had convened a special grand jury to investigate Loudoun County Public Schools. This meant that, for the next at least six months, school board members, administration officials, teachers, victims, and others would testify to a grand jury that could either indict for crimes, write a report detailing the failures of Loudoun County Public Schools, or both.

With that news and with the removal hearing approaching, I decided to take out a full-page ad in both local papers and just create a chronology of the facts behind the sexual assaults that occurred in 2021. By now other parent groups had formed in Loudoun County—Moms for Liberty, Army of Parents, Loudoun County Moms, and Virginia Overwatch. I invited them all to be a part of the ad, which would be so fact based and free from rhetoric that even the Loudoun for All clown show would be at a loss to "fact check" it. I wanted everything out there that we had found. I wanted the attorney general's office to see it. I wanted the public to see it. I wanted the school board and Superintendent Ziegler to see it. And now I want the country to see it:

PARENTS OF THE WORLD, UNITE!

INTENTIONAL COVER UP OR RECKLESS INDIFFERENCE AT LOUDOUN COUNTY PUBLIC SCHOOLS?

May 27, 2021
Loudoun County Public Schools suspends Tanner Cross for stating during a school board meeting's public comment session about proposed Policy 8040 (Rights of Transgender and Gender-Expansive Students) that he could not affirm that "a biological boy can be a girl and vice versa because it's against my religion." *- NY Post, May 28, 2021.*

May 28, 2021
Loudoun County Sheriff's Office is notified that a freshman girl at Stone Bridge High School was sexually assaulted by a boy in a girls' bathroom.
- Washington Post, October 25, 2021.

Superintendent Scott Ziegler emails the Loudoun County School Board that "a female student alleged that a male student sexually assaulted her in the restroom" at Stone Bridge High School. *- WTOP, October 21, 2021.*

June 8, 2021
The Loudoun County Circuit Court issues an order reinstating Tanner Cross and noted that LCPS's notice to his school community about his being placed on administrative leave was "an unnecessary and vindictive act." *- Court Order in Cross v. Loudoun County School Board, Scott A. Ziegler and Lucia Villa Sebastian, CL21-3254.*

June 22, 2021
Hundreds of Loudoun residents attend school board meeting where Policy 8040 is to be discussed. The overwhelming majority of residents who spoke opposed Policy 8040 and other school board policies.
- Loudoun County School Board Meeting, June 22, 2021 (18:43-1:33:10).

Residents were ejected from the board room after Scott Smith, father of the girl who was the victim of the May 28th sexual assault, was arrested. The school board reconvened without allowing residents back in and continued the meeting in violation of Virginia law. *- Loudoun Times-Mirror, May 2, 2022.*

LCPS Superintendent Scott Ziegler later falsely states during that meeting (while discussing and debating proposed Policy 8040): "To my knowledge, we don't have any records of assaults occurring in our restrooms." *- Daily Wire, October 11, 2021.*

School board sets August 10th meeting as date for vote on Policy 8040.
- Loudoun Now, June 23, 2021.

June 23, 2021
Scott Smith is issued a summons to appear in court on July 20, 2021 for a trial on charges of disorderly conduct and resisting arrest.
- Loudoun County District Court Docket GC21002081-00.

July 8, 2021
The assailant in the Stone Bridge sexual assault is arrested and charged the next day.
- FOX5, October 13, 2021.

July 16, 2021
LCPS does not comply with the deadline to file its legally mandated, annual Discipline, Crime, and Violence report, which includes reports of sexual assault.
- ABC7, May 3, 2022.

July 20, 2021
Scott Smith's trial date is continued to August 17, 2021 – 6 days after expected passage of Policy 8040. *- Loudoun County District Court Docket GC21002081-00.*

August 10, 2021
During public comment, Brenda Sheridan calls the name of the sexual assault victim's mother to speak. She does not appear, but Scott Ziegler writes a note and walks it over to Sheridan. Despite video evidence, LCPS neither produced the document nor offered any explanation for failing to produce it. *- LCPS Response to FOIA R000662-110921*

August 11, 2021
Policy 8040 passes with a 7-2 vote. *- Loudoun Times-Mirror, August 11, 2021.*

August 13, 2021
Two days after passing Policy 8040 and four weeks late, LCPS submits its Discipline, Crime, and Violence report. It does not include the Stone Bridge sexual assault in its submission. *- ABC7, May 3, 2022*

August 17, 2021
Commonwealth Attorney Buta Biberaj personally handles Scott Smith's criminal trial and he is convicted of disorderly conduct and resisting arrest.
- Loudoun Now, August 17, 2021.

August 26, 2021
Loudoun County Juvenile Court Services emails LCPS on the first day of school regarding the status of the Stone Bridge defendant. *- LCPS Response to FOIA R000707-112821*

October 7, 2021
A teenager is charged with sexual battery and abduction of a fellow student at Broad Run High School that occurred the previous day.
- Loudoun County Sheriff's Office Release, October 7, 2021.

October 11, 2021
The Daily Wire reports that the assailant at Broad Run was the same student that committed the sexual assault at Stone Bridge on May 28, 2021.
- Daily Wire, October 11, 2021.

October 14, 2021
The Virginia Department of Education emails LCPS asking why it did not include the Stone Bridge sexual assault in its Discipline, Crime, and Violence report.
- ABC7, May 3, 2022.

October 15, 2021
Loudoun County Public Schools decides to hire a law firm after seeing a news article stating that the Smith family would be filing a Title IX lawsuit against the division; LCPS ultimately tapped Blankingship & Keith due to the "threat of litigation."
- Fight for Schools v. Loudoun County Public Schools, Hearing Transcript, CL22-1462.

October 20, 2021
LCPS emails the VDOE and explains that it did not report the Stone Bridge sexual assault as required by law because it didn't start internally investigating the incident until October. The VDOE reminds LCPS that the law requires all incidents need to be reported when the police were notified, which occurred on May 28th. *- ABC7, May 3, 2022.*

November 4, 2021
Attorney General-elect Jason Miyares announces his office will investigate LCPS.
- Loudoun Times-Mirror, November 4, 2021.

November 5, 2021
Superintendent Ziegler announces that Blankingship & Keith will conduct an "independent review" of how LCPS handled the sexual assaults. LCPS continues to block the release the results of that review. *- ABC7, February 1, 2022.*

November 10, 2021
Sheriff Michael Chapman writes in a letter to Superintendent Ziegler that Loudoun County Juvenile Services Unit (JCSU) confirmed to LCSO that JSCU followed the law with respect to notifying LCPS that the defendant had been charged and that JSCU had contacted LCPS in late August to further discuss the defendant's court-ordered disposition *- "Letter from Sheriff Chapman to Scott Ziegler."*
JCSU confirmed in response to a FOIA that it follows the law with respect to VA Code §16.1-260(G), which requires the intake officer to file a report with the school division superintendent when a juvenile has been charged with sexual assault.
- Loudoun County Response to FOIA R010219-050522

January 15, 2022
Governor Glenn Youngkin authorizes the Office of the Attorney General to investigate Loudoun County Public Schools for its handling of the sexual assault.
- Executive Order Number Four, Authorizing an Investigation of Loudoun County Public Schools by the Attorney General, January 15, 2022.

April 7, 2022
A special grand jury is reportedly convened to investigate the Loudoun County school division's handling of the sexual assaults. *- Loudoun Now, April 4, 2022.*

Paid for by Army of Parents, Fight for Schools, Loudoun County Republican Womens' Club, Moms for Liberty – Loudoun County, Moms of Loudoun County, and VA Overwatch.
Not authorized by any candidate.

226

By July, Loudoun County Public Schools would be hit with two more lawsuits. After I had stood up for the two teachers at the school board meeting, they were called to testify before the grand jury. Then their contracts were not renewed despite a teacher shortage and one of the teachers having recently been given the special education teacher of the year award. When they went to the school board meeting in June to speak out about what they rightfully saw as retaliation, they were put on administrative leave for the rest of the year. The next week, one of the teachers filed her lawsuit in Loudoun County Circuit Court.

A week later, after months of preparation and hard work, America First Legal was able to file its lawsuit on behalf of 12 Loudoun County parents against LCPS for violating their constitutional and statutory parental rights for its implementation of critical race theory, social and emotional learning, Policy 8040.

Then in mid-July, Loudoun County Public Schools took the unusual step of trying to shut down the special grand jury by civilly suing the Virginia Office of the Attorney General. As always, the left seemed like maybe they knew something we didn't—they were overly confident that the grand jury would be shut down. When the time came for the hearing, however, our side once again packed the room and breathed a sigh of relief as the judge came to a swift and decisive decision to dismiss LCPS's Hail Mary and declare that the special grand jury would continue its work. LCPS tried again at the Virginia Supreme Court, and once more suffered a humiliating loss.

Finally, in September of 2022 Governor Youngkin rescinded the Virginia Department of Education Model Policy that required school districts to have policies in place that would force children to use bathrooms with members of the opposite sex, compel children and teachers to use the preferred pronouns of other children, and allow biological males to be able to play in girls sports. This model policy was the basis for Loudoun County Public Schools Policy 8040, and now it had to be scrapped.

In its place was a new model policy that school divisions would have to vote on at the local level. It defined sex as "biological sex." It clearly stated that teachers and students could not be compelled to use a students preferred pronouns, that locker rooms and other intimate facilities be divided by sex, that sports would be separated by sex, and that parents must be informed if their child were questioning their gender.

It was pretty much the exact opposite of Policy 8040 proving once more to LCPS and Chardonnay Antifa that yes, elections do have consequences. Now it will be up to Loudoun County Public Schools to implement this new policy, or face more angry parents in court.

How this all ends remains to be seen. But while the school board and the woke politicians were gaming the system to fight the shiny object of the Sheridan and Reaser removal cases, we opened up another front against them with litigation, requests for official action from the Youngkin administration, and independent outside support for a grand jury investigation.

The sitting members of the Loudoun County School Board had survived the removal cases, but they were the catalyst for a movement that helped elected Glenn Youngkin, Winsome Sears, and Jason Miyares. The result of that election turned into a grand jury investigation into criminal activity, while parents surrounded them with civil litigation that will have them explaining their actions in depositions for years.

They may not agree, but it's starting to look like the best thing that could have happened for some of these school board members would have been being removed from office.

THE MOST IMPORTANT THING

Throughout this book, I have outlined the way in which parents fought back against their woke school system in Loudoun County. The way we operated was crucial to our success. But as important as those things are, there is one thing that is more important than that.

We are parents, and we will fight to the ends of the earth for our children.

I will never forget when my daughters were born and their tiny hands tightly grabbed by thumb. Since those moments, I have made it my life's mission to keep them safe from harm, to guide them through childhood, to teach them the lessons that I learned from my parents and my experiences, and to turn them into kind, compassionate, and mentally tough individuals who can handle whatever life throws at them.

That is what we do as parents. It is, of course, not an exact science. No two people are alike, and despite our attempts to shape our children a certain way, they will also be a product of their time, not ours. As much as I would love them to watch the same movies as me, follow the same sports teams, read the same books, and have the same joys that I did as a child, they live in a different world and will have different experiences that will shape who they are to become. That applies to all parents today.

But what we can do is to ensure that they believe in the American Dream, will help those who need help, judge people by the content of their character, and are critical thinkers who value reason, science, literature, art, and history and know the positives and negatives of human nature and how that has impacted civilizations throughout time.

We certainly cannot do that alone, so it requires a level of trust. When we let our children sleep over a friend's house, we must first trust the friend's parents. When we hire a babysitter, we must trust that person with the responsibility for our children, even if for a few hours. When we send our children to camp, we must trust that it is a good organization with good people running it. All of these things require us to make judgments before we can exercise that trust, so we do our homework, check references, and make the best decisions that we can with the information we have been provided. Sometimes, even if we have no reason to doubt the safety of our children, our instincts tell us something is off, so we follow that instinct, telling ourselves that it's better to be safe than sorry.

For years, we have reflexively trusted our public schools. We believed that when we sent our children through the school doors every morning that the school would take seriously the responsibility we had bestowed upon them. That our children's teachers would understand that their limited mandate was not to inculcate morals or contradict what the parents did, but rather to assist us in teaching our children math, science, reading, writing, and history. We have expected that our children might be disciplined in school but that such discipline would be meted out fairly. We believed that our elected school board members would represent us to ensure that our schools focused on this mission and that they would not use their positions to advance their political careers or indoctrinate our children in one political ideology or another.

Unfortunately, that is no longer what our public schools are about. Maybe they never were. There are certainly people that have been ringing the alarm bell for years, decades even. But as parents, we were so wrapped up in providing for our families and giving our children a good home that we naively assumed that our schools were responsibly exercising the authority we had delegated to them.

It took a pandemic to wake us all out of our slumber. As we worked from home while our children learned from home, we saw that schools remained closed because of politics. Then we learned that what our children were learning veered way off course. They were learning that they were either victims or oppressors, that boys could become girls and girls could become boys, and that to believe otherwise made them intolerant, bigoted, and not worthy of approval in today's society. They were being taught that our country was irredeemably racist and that the morals of a civilized society in the 21st century should be applied to every period throughout history, making any historical figure of the past subject to cancellation and ignominy.

When our children returned to school, they were told that they would need to learn new pronouns and refer to each other by such pronouns. They were required to share bathrooms and locker rooms with members of the opposite sex regardless of safety risks or privacy concerns. And we were told that we had no right to know if our children had succumbed to a social contagion and wanted to identify as a member of the opposite sex while at school. If we had a problem with that, the schools would make it incredibly difficult for us to do anything about it beyond pulling our children from public schools.

In essence, the schools were telling us that our core function as parents—to be the primary decision maker with respect to the health, welfare, and education of our children—would now be shared with the government.

What these school systems failed to realize was that as parents, when our newborn babies first grasped our thumb, we were hit with more than love and the realization that we would be responsible for guiding our children throughout their lives. In their blind arrogance that "they know best," they forgot that when our children were born, we also found ourselves receiving something not unlike the gamma rays that comic book hero Bruce Banner received. Sure, he remained a mild-mannered scientist most of the time, as we parents do. But like him, "you wouldn't like us when we're angry." Whereas he turned into the Incredible Hulk, we turned into the incredible parents fighting for our children's souls.

Loudoun County became ground zero for that fight, and parents were able to channel that anger and instinctive need to protect their children into a plan of action that, not only had game-changing political consequences in Virginia, but also served as a beacon of hope for the rest of the country.

Now the parents' revolution is growing and evolving. Parents everywhere are standing up, refusing to back down, and making changes locally, at the state level, and hopefully after 2024 at the federal level. Organizations are forming to help those parents become more informed about what is happening in schools around the country, while other groups have stepped up to provide legal assistance to those brave souls seeking to enforce their fundamental rights as parents.

This is a fight to stop schools from taking over the role of parents; to respect the limited mandate of schools to educate children in math, science, reading, writing, and history; to end the war on critical thinking in favor of a one-size-fits-all approach where everyone must conform; and to make our system of education the best in the world so that our children will be able to compete in a time where their knowledge and experience will take them places we no longer can.

To do this, we must fight smarter, harder, and more effectively than our opponents. We must not give in to the baser tendencies of hate and anger, but rather demonstrate to our children and the world that the rule of law, rationalism, critical thinking, and strategic action can still win in the United States of America.

This is a fight for our children, for our families, and for the values that will propel us as a nation to be a more perfect union. It is the fight of our lives.

Be the hero for your children that you were meant to be...and go win it.

ACKNOWLEDGMENTS

To everyone who served with me in this fight: you have been an inspiration to millions of parents across this great nation. When you look back on all that you have accomplished in life, you will know that you changed the course of history and your place in the resurrection of this place we call America is secure for eternity. I would like to give extra thanks to the following people for their herculean efforts: Amy Jahr, Erin Dunbar, Sandra Vaughn, Jessica Mendez, Michael Primazon, Erin Brown, Emily Curtis, Stacy Markus, Beth Hess, Darris Hess, Michael Rivera, Mike Biron, Elicia Brand, Suzanne Satterfield, Jamie Fortier, Laura Johnson, Michele Mege, Kate O'Hara, Colin Doninger, Ronda Nassib, Kay Greenwell, Cheryl Onderchain, Erin Smith, Emily Emschwiller, Sharon Virts, John Whitbeck, Patti Menders, Debbie Rose, Jeremy Wright, Carri Michon, Abbie Platt, Emily Borkholder, Anne Miller, Debbie Edsall, Shelly Shlebrch, Jonathan Erickson, Karlee Copeland, Elizabeth Perrin, Nick Mozer (and the goons), and Joe Mobley.

NOTES

PROLOGUE:
THE BREAKING POINT

1 Luke Rosiak, "Loudoun County Schools Tried to Conceal Sexual Assault against Daughter in Bathroom, Father Says," *The Daily Wire*, https://www.dailywire.com/news/loudoun-county-schools-tried-to -conceal-sexual-assault-against-daughter-in-bathroom-father-says.

2 Ibid.

RULE NO. 1:
EVERY NEIGHBORHOOD IS A BATTLEFIELD

1 Ian Prior, "Trump Right to Order Fed Investigation of Floyd Death in Minneapolis—Here's What Could Happen Now," Fox News, May 29, 2020, https://www.foxnews.com/opinion/ian-prior-trump-right-to-order -fed-investigation-of-floyd-death-in-minneapolis-heres-what-could -happen-now.

RULE NO. 2:
ACTIVATE, INVESTIGATE, COMMUNICATE

1 Ibid.

2 Almanzan, J., Meyer, G., and Johnson, A., *Introduction to Critical Race Theory*. Retrieved on October 11, 2022 from https://theequitycollaborative. com/wp-content/uploads/2020/05/Intro-To-Critical-Race-Theory.pdf.

3 Veronike Collazo, "For Black History Month, This Loudoun County Elementary School Played a Runaway Slave 'Game' in Gym Class," *The*

Loudoun Daily Mirror, February 21, 2019, https://www.loudountimes
.com/news/for-black-history-month-this-loudoun-county-elementary
-school-played-a-runaway-slave-game-in/article_9cecd568-35ef-11e9
-8540-6372d03d3025.html.

4 Nikole Hannah-Jones, "The 1619 Project," *The New York Times*, August 14,
2019, https://www.nytimes.com/interactive/2019/08/14/magazine/1619
-america-slavery.html.

5 Mark Moore, "Trump Expands Ban on Critical Race Theory to Federal
Contractors," *The New York Post,* September 23, 2020, https://nypost
.com/2020/09/23/trump-expands-ban-on-critical-race-theory-to-federal
-contractors/.

RULE NO. 3:
ALWAYS FLIP THE SCRIPT

1 Jonathan Haidt, "Why the Past 10 Years of American Life Have
Been Uniquely Stupid," *The Atlantic*, April 11, 2022, https://www
.theatlantic.com/magazine/archive/2022/05/social-media-democracy
-trust-babel/629369/.

2 Justin Moyer, "Drunk Wives Matter T-Shirt Pulled at Virginia Restaurant amid Uproar," *The Washington Post,* June 16, 2020, https://www
.washingtonpost.com/dc-md-va/2020/06/16/drunk-wives-matter-t-shirt
-pulled-virginia-restaurant-amid-uproar/.

3 Luke Rosiak, "Teachers Compile List Of Parents Who Question
Racial Curriculum, Plot War On Them," *The Daily Wire,* https://www
.dailywire.com/news/loudoun-teachers-target-parents-critical-race
-theory-hacking.

RULE NO. 4:
IDENTIFY THE "BAD GUYS" AND TAKE IT TO 'EM

1 John Battison, Barts reprimanded from School Board for disclosing
confidential info, *Loudoun Times-Mirror,* https://www.loudountimes
.com/news/barts-reprimanded-from-school-board-for-disclosing-confi
dential-info/article_dca4b148-29be-11eb-ba31-03bc1c90f764.html.

2 Loudoun Now Staff, Following Censure Vote, Barts Loses Committee
Seats, *Loudoun Now,* https://www.loudounnow.com/2021/03/10/following
-censure-vote-barts-loses-committee-seats/

3 Loudoun County School Board Policy 1030, A Code of Conduct for School Board Members, May 8, 1973.

RULE NO. 5:
TURN YOUR FIGHT INTO MUST-SEE TV

1 Sam Dorman, "Virginia Parents Group Launches PAC to Unseat School Board Members over Reopening, Race Controversies," Fox News, April 13, 2021, https://www.foxnews.com/politics/virginia-parents-pac -school-board-members-reopening-critical-race-theory.

RULE NO. 6:
DO NOT GET STUCK IN THE MUD

1 https://loudounnow.com/wp-content/uploads/2021/05/Draft-POLICY_ -8040-Rights-of-Transgender-Students-5-6-21.pdf
2 Ibid.
3 Ezra Marcus, "A Guide to Neopronouns," *The New York Times*, April 8, 2021, https://www.nytimes.com/2021/04/08/style/neopronouns-nonbinary -explainer.html.
4 Ibid.

RULE NO. 7:
WHEN THEY MOBILIZE, GO GUERRILLA

1 Luke Rosiak, "Loudoun County Schools Tried to Conceal Sexual Assault against Daughter in Bathroom, Father Says," *The Daily Wire*, https://www.dailywire.com/news/loudoun-county-schools-tried-to -conceal-sexual-assault-against-daughter-in-bathroom-father-says.
2 Jay Cuasay, "My School Board Is under Attack and Soon Yours Might Be Too," dailykos.com, June 23, 2021, https://www.dailykos .com/stories/2021/6/23/2036664/-My-school-board-is-under-attack -and-soon-yours-might-be-too.

RULE NO. 8:
DO NOT STOP AT THE WALL

1 Nick Givas, "CNN Slights Mount Rushmore as 'Monument of Two Slaveowners' after Extolling Its 'Majesty' in 2016," July 3, 2020, https://www.foxnews.com/media/cnn-mount-rushmore-monument -two-slave-owners.

2 Ron Elving, "Reflections on a 4th That Seems Far from Glorious," NPR, July 3, 2020, https://www.npr.org/2020/07/03/886523793/reflection -on-a-4th-that-seems-far-from-glorious.

RULE NO. 9:
YOU'VE GOTTA BELIEVE

1 Attorney General Merrick Garland, "Partnership among Federal, State, Local, Tribal, and Territorial Law Enforcement to Address Threats against School Administrators, Board Members, Teachers, and Staff," October 4, 2021, https://www.mdjonline.com/garland-memo/pdf _01521414-26b6-11ec-a064-ff37c7337c32.html.

2 Full NSBA Letter to Biden Administration and Department of Justice Memo—Parents Defending Education, https://defendinged.org/press -releases/full-nsba-letter-to-biden-administration-and-department-of -justice-memo/.

3 Luke Rosiak, "Loudoun County Schools Tried to Conceal Sexual Assault against Daughter in Bathroom, Father Says," *The Daily Wire*, https:// www.dailywire.com/news/loudoun-county-schools-tried-to-conceal -sexual-assault-against-daughter-in-bathroom-father-says.

RULE NO. 10:
DON'T LET 'EM OFF THE ROPES

1 Paul LeBlanc, "Juli Briskman, Cyclist Who Flipped Off Trump Motor-cade, Wins Local Office in Virginia," CNN Politics, November 6, 2019, https://www.cnn.com/2019/11/05/politics/juli-briskman-trump-motor cade-flipped-off-local-office-win/index.html.

RULE NO. 11:
DON'T BE OVERLY RELIANT ON PAST SUCCESS

1 Kevin Daley, "Soros Prosecutor under Fire for Mishandling Child Endan-germent, Domestic Abuse Cases," freebeacon.com, October 4, 2021, https://freebeacon.com/democrats/brutal-domestic-homicide-spars -backlash-against-soros-prosecutor/.

2 Chrissy Clark, "Loudoun County Sheriff Blasts Public School Super-intendent: He Was 'Unmistakably Aware' of Rape Accusation," *The Daily Caller*, November 22, 2021, https://dailycaller.com/2021/11/22 /loudoun-county-sheriff-blasts-public-school-superintendent-he-was -unmistakably-aware-of-rape-accusations/.

3 Alex Nester and Matthew Foldi, "Soros-Backed Attorney Kills Effort to Recall School Board Member Who Fought Reopening," freebeacon .com, August 27, 2021, https://freebeacon.com/campus/soros-backed -attorney-kills-effort-to-recall-school-board-member-who-fought -reopening/.

4 Harold Hutchinson, "NAACP Chapter Accuses Parents of Racism for Trying to Recall School Board Members Who Covered Up In-School Sexual Assaults," *The Daily Caller*, January 19, 2022, https://dailycaller .com/2022/01/19/naalp-loudoun-school-board-sexual-assault-racism/.

RULE NO. 12:
PLAY THE ENDGAME

1 Nathaniel Cline, "Virginia Attorney General-Elect Miyares Plans to Investigate School Assault Cases in Loudoun; Chief Prosecutor Welcomes Involvement," November 4, 2021, loudountimes.com, https://www.loudountimes.com/news/virginia-attorney-general-elect -miyares-plans-to-investigate-school-assault-cases-in-loudoun-chief -prosecutor/article_51ed0f00-3dd6-11ec-a6c7-339513c0a478.html#:~:text =Virginia%20Attorney%20General-elect%20Jason%20S.%20 Miyares%20%28R%29%20said,the%20prosecutors%20are%20 not%20doing%20an%20adequate%20job.

2 "LCPS Announces Independent Review of Assault Allegations." *Loudoun County Public Schools*, November 5, 2021. Press release.

3 Office of Governor Glenn Youngkin, "Governor Glenn Youngkin Signs 11 Day One Executive Actions," Governor Glenn Youngkin, https://www .governor.virginia.gov/news-releases/2022/january/name-918519-en. html.

4 4- EO 4 Executive Order 4 on Loudoun County Investigation.docx, https:// www.governor.virginia.gov/media/governorvirginiagov/governor -of-virginia/pdf/74---eo/74---eo/EO-4-Executive-Order-4-on --Loudoun-County-Investigation.pdf.

5 *Barnett et. al. v. Loudoun County School Board*, CL-22-546 (transcript of February 17, 2022, hearing).

6 Nick Minock, "Loudoun Parent Group Wants Youngkin's Office to Remove Superintendent for 'Dishonesty,'" ABC7 News, https://wjla .com/news/crisis-in-the-classrooms/loudoun-county-public-schools -fight-for-schools-parents-glenn-youngkin-jillian-barrow-remove -superintendent-dr-scott-ziegler.

7 Hannah Natanson, "Jillian Balow Says the Virginia Board of Education Is Looking into Allegations against Loudoun County Public Schools Superintendent Scott Ziegler," *The Washington Post*, March 22, 2022, https://www.washingtonpost.com/education/2022/03/22/balow-letter-superintendent-loudoun/.

8 "Parents Prevail in Freedom of Information Act Case against Loudoun Schools," DC Presswire, May 22, 2022, https://www.dcpresswire.com/article/570681645-parents-prevail-in-freedom-of-information-act-case-against-loudoun-schools.

ABOUT THE AUTHOR

an Prior is one of the most recognizable voices in the parents' revolution that has swept the country. Ian began his career as an attorney in New England in 2002 after graduating from Boston University School of Law. He transitioned into politics in 2011, working on various Republican campaigns before serving as a top spokesman at the Justice Department. Ian is married and has two daughters in elementary school in Loudoun County Public Schools in Virginia. In 2021, Ian formed the group Fight for Schools.